It's a God Thing!

Tonya Hance

Published by Tonya's Captured Inspirations LLC

Any italics in the Scripture quotations reflect the author's own emphasis.

Some of the names in this book have been changed out of respect for the privacy of the individuals mentioned.

ISBN-13: 978-0-6925-9089-8
ISBN-10: 0-6925-9089-7

This book is dedicated to my mother, Betty Hance, who passed away on November 14, 2015, during the editing of this book. I will always be grateful for the spiritual foundation she gave me as a young child.

ACKNOWLEDGMENTS

Thank you God for saving me by your grace and drawing me closer to You each and every day. Thank You for giving me the inspiration behind this book and the spiritual analogies to share.

A special thank you to my mother, Betty Hance, for living a life for Christ and setting a spiritual foundation for me as a young child.

Thank you to the real "Hannah" who preferred her name to not be mentioned in this book because she wanted all credit to go to God. You are truly beautiful on the inside and out! Thank you for being "God's girl" and for investing in me!

Thank you to the real "Josh and Katy" who also preferred their names to not be mentioned in this book. You have both been spiritual influences on me, and I am grateful for the time you spent investing in me.

Thank you to my editor, Camilla Palmer LoJeske, for giving your time and helping to make this book possible. I appreciated every yellow highlight!

Thank you Julie Seat of Longs Peak Web Design (www.longspeakweb.com) for designing my website and setting up my blog.

Thank you to all who encouraged me to put my writings into a book!

ABOUT THE AUTHOR

Tonya Hance is a Christian speaker, photographer, and writer who shares her love for God through spiritual analogies. She is passionate about hiking, caving, canyoneering, and exploring God's awesome world. She has a strong interest in discovering and photographing historical and archaeological remnants such as ghost towns, mining camps, and ancient Anasazi ruins. In addition to owning a small landscape and portrait photography business, Tonya is also a nanny and loves to share her joy and knowledge of the outdoors with children by leading them on hiking and caving expeditions.

Tonya also travels to various churches and events presenting a program entitled, "Step Into the Light", in which she incorporates caving analogies to help lead people to Christ by operating on the premise that without Jesus one lives in a spiritual cave of darkness. By combining caving techniques and Biblical references as analogies, she shows the audience their need for Christ's light in their lives.

This presentation is a result of her own spiritual journey of being stuck in a dark, hopeless place to experiencing the light and freedom of God's love. Tonya spent many years of her life as a painfully shy and withdrawn social recluse trapped behind strongholds and walls she had erected. She is a living example of how God can change people from the inside out, make beauty from ashes, and totally transform lives. Her favorite Bible verse is Philippians 4:13, "I can do all things through Christ who gives me strength."

To sign up for Tonya's blog and view her photography, please visit her website at www.tonyascapturedinspirations.com. Her blog is located on her website under the heading, "Adventures with Tonya". She may be contacted via e-mail at tonya@tonyascapturedinspirations.com.

Table of Contents

The Prelude

Part 1: My Story

Chapter 1: The Beginning

Chapter 2: The Rebel

Chapter 3: The Power of Prayer

Chapter 4: The Prayer Partner

Chapter 5: The Flood

Chapter 6: The Call to Serve

Part 2: God Moments

Chapter 1: Stranded in Kentucky

Chapter 2: Alone in the Wilderness

Chapter 3: Trick Riding

Chapter 4: Herding Cattle in the Canyon

Chapter 5: Saying No to Kings

Chapter 6: The Sand Trap

Chapter 7: Peace in the Storm

Chapter 8: Blurred Vision

Part 3: The Analogies

Chapter 1: Let God be Your Belayer

Chapter 2: Things Aren't Always What They Seem

Chapter 3: Dance in the Rain

Chapter 4: Memorials in our lives

Chapter 5: Spiritual Bullfighting

Chapter 6: Lessons from a Train Ride

Chapter 7: Settling at Good Enough

Chapter 8: Fickle Behavior

Chapter 9: Acceptance

Chapter 10: The Blame Game

Chapter 11: Grace

Chapter 12: Making the Impossible Possible

Part 4: Epilogue

Chapter 1: Seeing God in the Pain

Chapter 2: The Road to Salvation

The Prelude

Several years ago, a friend and I went on a caving expedition. We drove several miles on a remote, dirt road until the road deteriorated into higher clearance conditions than my vehicle would allow. We then hiked for two hours up and down steep hills for the next few miles in the hot, morning sun before stepping off the road onto a faint path in the trees. We followed this overgrown path for about two miles to the cave entrance surprising a bull along the way. By his pawing stance and snorts, he did not seem very happy about our intrusion. After caving for about seven hours, we began the long trek back to my vehicle. Covered in mud from head to toe, we placed one tired, weary foot in front of the other. The sun was beginning to set, and we were nervous about the prospect of encountering the bull in the dark.

"Wouldn't it be great if some people riding ATVs are there when we emerge from the trees and offer us a ride?" I asked my friend.

I knew that the chances of that happening at any time in this remote area, but especially at this time of the evening, were slim. My friend realized that too, but we dreamed about it anyway.

"Sure," she responded despondently.

Caving is a very physical activity. We were beyond the point of exhaustion after a five mile hike just to reach the cave plus seven hours of caving. My friend and I put one weary foot in front of the other, over and over, through the seemingly never ending forest. The sky was beginning to grow dim as we finally emerged from the trees onto the dirt road and saw, to our surprise, four elderly people standing next to two ATVs! One was a traditional ATV while the other was a Side by Side UTV. My friend and I looked at each other in astonishment as one of the men asked,

"Do you girls need a ride?"

He then added, "There are a lot of mountain lions hunting out here this time of evening."

As I glanced at the man, my mouth dropped open in amazement and chills ran over my body for he was wearing a ball cap that stated, "It's a God thing!"

My friend and I looked at each other and quickly nodded agreement to the offer of a ride. One of the elderly women hopped into the Side by Side with the other couple leaving my friend and I riding triple on the traditional ATV with the elderly gentleman who had offered us the ride. It is not the safest scenario to ride triple on an ATV. However, my friend and I were both fairly skinny at the time. Besides, the man was wearing a hat that said, "It's a God thing". We figured we would be okay! The headlamps on the ATVs lit the way in the evening gloom as we made our way up that rugged, mountain road. My friend and I stifled a giggle when the woman driving the Side by Side got to a particularly rough portion of the road because she had a huge smile on her face as she gunned the engine up it. I thought to myself, "I want to be cool like her when I get old one day, still out living life!"

Our ATV angels brought us back to my vehicle then offered an invitation to stop by their house on our way home for a shower and a late dinner. We were absolutely disgusting looking after a hard day of caving, yet these kind people invited us into their home. My friend and I accepted their invitation, and after cleaning up, enjoyed a nice meal with them. The couple shared that they were Seventh Day Adventist Christians who want everyone they encounter to see Jesus in them. They not only made us feel welcome that night, but they also invited us to come back anytime and showed us their spare bedrooms.

While I was praying about the title to this book, God reminded me of this story and of the man's hat proclaiming, "It's a God thing!" We are quick to say that so many of our chance encounters in life are just coincidences, but in truth, they are divine appointments by God. They are God things! Meeting those elderly people that evening was a God thing. It was an answer to a prayer that we didn't even pray but God knew we needed. That is what this book is about: God moments, divine appointments, God things! I pray that you will be blessed, inspired, and encouraged as you read of personal experiences in my life and spiritual analogies that God has given me to share.

Part 1: My Story

Chapter 1: The Beginning

Our lives are tapestries interwoven by interactions with others who have left their footprints on our hearts. My story began in a hospital in Memphis, Tennessee, on a fall morning. My parents had been told that they wouldn't be able to have children, so they adopted my brother. Then, I came along. Surprise! A few years later, my younger brother made a surprise entry as well. I guess the doctors aren't always right!

My mom was the spiritual leader in our family. My dad believed in God; my mom made sure he accepted Christ before she married him. However, by the time I was in second grade, he had given up on church after being burned by some church members. Week after week, he stayed home watching television while my mom dragged all three of us kids to church. We were Southern Baptist which meant that we attended Sunday School and worship service on Sunday morning then came back on Sunday night for Discipleship Training followed by an evening service. As if that weren't enough, Wednesday evenings consisted of prayer meetings for the adults and more classes for us kids. Friday night was youth group. Yes, you guessed it, my mama made sure we were at church any time those doors were open! To top that off, my mom was the janitor for the church, so we were also there on Tuesday nights.

I resented having to go to church so much. It didn't seem fair that I had to go to church while my dad got to stay at home and watch television. The kids there weren't nice to me. I also hated the fact that I had to dress up. I couldn't stand to wear dresses. Each week, I fought a battle with my mom over having to wear a dress. She won every time, but I still fought my hardest. Church was boring and not fun. The sermons seemed to drag on and on. This particular church favored the hymn, "Just As I Am", and tended to labor slowly over every stanza of it while waiting for someone to finally walk the aisle during the invitation. I wanted to walk it just so the song would finally end!

I found ways to humor myself though. The church had an attendance board posted in the sanctuary next to the baptismal. Each week, some little old ladies faithfully recorded the number in attendance during morning and evening classes and services. I started playing around with the numbers changing the 60 in attendance for Discipleship Training to 600 and changing the 150 in attendance during morning worship to 50. Then, I sat back to watch the reaction! The little old ladies had no idea what had happened to their precious numbers and quickly worked to change them back to the records of the day. The next week, I struck again and continued to change their numbers over a period of months. I got the biggest kick out of messing with their attendance board. Nobody suspected me because I was the very quiet, shy child!

My mom made sure that her children knew the Bible through and through. We practiced Bible verses constantly. When I was in trouble, in addition to a whipping, she made me write Bible verses over and over. She wanted God's Word drilled into my head. She even made us do Bible studies with her during summer break. I remember sitting around the kitchen table with her and my brothers when I was nine years old as she told us that we were all sinners. "I am NOT a sinner!" I declared, not really understanding what that meant. The more she told me that I was indeed a sinner, the more I protested. I thought I was a little angel!

In the Bible Belt, fire and brimstone preaching was very popular during that time. "Choose God or burn in hell!" was a common phrase I heard preached. Graphic descriptions of burning in hell fire forever and ever convinced me to choose God when I was eleven years old. Sitting on hard church pews and singing endless hymns for eternity did not sound pleasant to me, but it sounded better than an everlasting fire. I didn't understand the "God is love" part. I chose Him out of fear.

Chapter 2: The Rebel

I have always been somewhat of a rebel; I like to go against the mainstream. As a child, I adamantly refused to wear a dress like the other girls my age at church. I was a tomboy and proud of it. When I was inducted into the National Junior Honor Society in sixth grade, the requirement for the ceremony was that everyone wear formal attire. That meant that the girls had to wear dresses.

"I just won't go!" I told my parents.

"You will go, and you will wear a dress!" they responded.

I went, unhappily, to the ceremony, sat on the front row of seats which faced the parents in the gym, and spread my legs open as wide as could be to my parents' horror. My mom's face turned bright red as she rapidly made hand motions to close my legs, which I pretended not to understand. I knew I was going to get it later, but this little form of rebellion for being forced to wear the hated dress was worth it for me. I smirked as I sat through the ceremony.

"Nobody is going to make me do anything I don't want to do!" I thought.

I paid for that little rebellion with a whipping and the punishment of having to wear a dress to school for a month. This punishment would have been devastating except that I quickly found a way around it. I wore a dress as commanded when I left the house, but I had pants hidden inside my backpack. I was one of the first on the school bus, so I quickly put the pants on and pulled the dress off. I wore a t-shirt underneath, so it wasn't like I was completely stripping. Sometimes, I wore jogging pants rolled up underneath a skirt. When I got on the bus, I pulled the pants down and the skirt off. This worked well until my pants began to slide down my leg one day as I got off the bus and walked up the driveway with my brothers. They tattled of course!

This rebellious attitude continued to plague me for many years. I couldn't stand for anyone to tell me what to do. I chose to attend a Bible College because I was offered free pizza and a full scholarship, but I hated the fact that chapel attendance there was mandatory. I, of course, found a way around it. I entered the chapel, checked in, then pretended to go to the bathroom and never came back. I ended up going to the movie theater or driving across the nearby state line to Mississippi to gamble on the riverboat barges during chapel time instead. I didn't feel like I fit into the pious church crowd. I liked my music loud, and above all else, I just wanted to have fun with no restrictions.

God was not fun to me. In fact, He seemed like the ultimate disciplinarian. One of my childhood punishments was to repeatedly write a verse of Scripture. Carbon paper became my solution to that! I could have several pages of handwritten Scripture by using one sheet of carbon paper. Sometimes, I even inserted two sheets of carbon paper between five pages. This multiplied my writings, yet it didn't ease my anger against God for having to write pieces of His boring book.

God represented punishment to me. I saw Him as essentially just words on a page and as religious motions to follow. I didn't see Him as anything positive. I didn't understand when people talked about having a relationship with Him. I didn't understand when people prayed like He truly would answer and like He actually cared. I believed in Him; I just didn't believe He really cared about His people. If He truly cared, why didn't He relieve the suffering in the world? I decided that He was an aloof God who wanted to be sung endless hymns for eternity and would strike down anyone who messed up.

I eventually quit college my senior year and moved to Colorado. All I had left to finish was my student teaching. I didn't know what I wanted to do in life, but I knew that being in a classroom day in and day out was not for me. I got a job waiting tables and loved the fast money that brought in. I bought myself a fully loaded Mustang right off the lot and began to explore the nearby hiking trails.

I didn't picture God as loving. In fact, I perceived that Jesus may love me, but God the Father sure hated me! I carried that perception around for a long time until God gave me a wakeup call one day with a moose encounter. I had prayed for a sign that God actually cared about me, a sign that He is more than just words on a page. God answered that prayer by having a moose stop me in my tracks and showed me through that experience that He was real. At that point, I believed He cared, but I still pictured Him as more of a stern, disapproving disciplinarian taking delight in punishing me than a loving Father who had given His only Son for my sake.

However, God sought to change my attitude about Him, and He began to put people in my path starting with an Adventist pastor named Josh. I received a small postcard in the mail that advertised a free Bible study about two weeks before the moose encounter. After that experience, I was ready to get to know God better and wanted to understand what a true relationship with Him looked like. I filled out the postcard thinking that the study would be delivered in the mail. Instead, a man named Josh showed up at my apartment door two weeks later.

"I'm here to do a Bible study with you," he said with a smile as I cautiously opened up my door at his knock. He explained that the card I had filled out was for an in-person Bible study.

"I'm not interested in doing this with you," I said. "But, I will take the study to do on my own."

Josh was very persistent, however, and thought that I might be more agreeable to allowing him in if he came back with a woman, so he made an appointment for the following week. I just wanted him off of my doorstep, so I agreed, although I had no intention of keeping the appointment.

The following week, there was another knock at my door. I had forgotten about Josh's appointment with me and my plan to avoid him. I opened the door out of habit. Josh was back, this time with a woman named Ruth. The two talked their way inside, and we began to go through their studies. They quickly realized that I, with my Bible education background, was way ahead of the content of their studies, so we decided to do an in-depth study of the book of John instead. Meanwhile, those two began to invite others who had filled out the Bible study postcards to my home. Soon, I was hosting a weekly Bible study!

In addition to being a rebel, I was a loner. I didn't have any close friends. Blame it on low self-esteem, poor self-image, shyness, social anxiety, or any number of things, but the fact remained that I was friendless. Suddenly people were coming to my home on a weekly basis, and I didn't know what to do with them! In all honesty, I was a terrible hostess! I never once offered anyone anything to eat or drink. I just sat there in shock week after week that people were coming over to my apartment for this study. The study eventually phased out. Josh moved away to another part of the state, and the Bible study was over just as quickly as it had begun. But, Josh had taught me a little of what Christian fellowship looked like through those studies. It wasn't about putting on a pious act in church. It wasn't about dressing a certain way. It wasn't even about knowing tons of Scripture. Christian fellowship was about growing together in Christ.

Shortly after Josh moved, the church that I attended, which was not the church that he pastored, began to have some serious problems. There were major fights about music and money. It got to the point that I didn't want to be around that negativity, so I stopped going. I attempted to find a new church to attend, but just like the Israelites when they left Egypt, I longed for the past. I couldn't find a new church that I liked that had familiar faces or a potluck once a month, so I just didn't attend worship services anymore. However, I did become involved with a weekly, women's Bible study.

A couple of years later, Josh and his family came back to town for a weekend. His wife, Katy, invited me to a presentation some members of their new congregation were doing in a local Adventist church. She asked me to do her a favor and sit by her youngest son during it as she was part of the presentation. This church happened to be close to where I lived, so I walked there, in a t-shirt and shorts, the rebel in me determined not to conform to what I considered pious religious dress codes. Suspiciously enough, once I got there, Katy no longer had a need for child care assistance. I sat there in the pew studying her as she prepared with her group while wondering if the childcare thing was a ruse to get me to come to church, something that I had given up on. Soon, her group began their presentation about prayer and God moments. They were huge on prayer and asked everyone to take turns praying with one of the four of them at the end. I declined and made my way over to the luncheon area.

I didn't buy into the prayer thing. It seemed like a cop-out to me. When I overheard people stating that they would pray about something, my first thought was,

"Why don't you get your lazy butt up and do something to help the situation instead?"

I didn't understand the power of prayer. It seemed like a last resort to me. After all, Jesus might love me, but God the Father sure hated me! Everyone at the luncheon was friendly, and it was great to meet up with Josh and Katy again, both of whom I looked up to greatly for investing time with me in the past. During that visit, Josh invited me to a prayer conference he was holding at his church that fall. A prayer conference did not sound exciting to me in the least, but, out of respect for him, I agreed to attend while inwardly rolling my eyes at the thought of a long, boring weekend solely focused on prayer.

I attended his prayer conference that fall, and what I thought was going to be an incredibly boring weekend ended up changing my life and my attitudes about prayer.

Chapter 3: The Power of Prayer

At this point in my spiritual walk, I was totally into Jesus, but I wasn't so sure about God. Since I had read the entire Bible several times and studied it in-depth in Bible college, I had a tendency to overanalyze passages and found several that seemed to affirm my concept of God as a stern, mean, disciplinarian who couldn't wait to punish those who messed up. I arrived at Josh's church shortly before the prayer conference began, dressed casually of course and mentally rolling my eyes at the thought of spending two and a half days in prayer. It literally seemed like torture to me!

The conference opened up in popcorn prayer – something I had never heard of before. This meant that people randomly said praises to God such as "You are awesome; You are mighty". This popcorn prayer seemed to last for eternity, although in truth it was probably for only about ten minutes. Next, everyone got in small groups and prayed specifically for different topics, each topic for about ten minutes. I didn't pray aloud, so I remained silent the whole time wondering when we were going to have a break and eat. Finally, the prayer time ended, and we were given a choice of several classes to attend. Not having paid attention to the class choices, I attended a class solely based on its name, the

Muskoxes, because it sounded funny. I had no idea what I was getting myself into!

The class I chose began with a really cool wildlife video, found on YouTube, entitled "The Battle at Kruger". This video included raw footage, taken by a couple on a safari, of lions attacking a baby water buffalo that had wandered away from most of its herd. The video first showed some lions waiting on the opportunity to pounce on the baby, and then it graphically portrayed the attack. The few water buffalo that were with the baby fled leaving it to fight the battle alone. I cringed as the ferocious lions tugged on the baby near some water. Just when I thought things couldn't get worse, a crocodile joined in on the attack! The situation seemed hopeless.

As I watched this, I totally identified with the baby water buffalo. I was used to fighting my battles alone. I was used to friends deserting me when times were tough. I was used to things being bad and of a "crocodile" joining the fight to drag me down when I thought things couldn't possibly get any worse. I nodded my head throughout this portion of the video. I understood what this battle was about. I knew what it was like to fight battles alone.

The next part of the video surprised me, however. I thought the baby water buffalo was done for. After all, how could it possibly survive an attack by several lions AND a crocodile? The situation seemed impossible to me. Suddenly, a massive herd of water buffalo came to the rescue and literally sent the lions flying with some sound kicks and head butts. The few water buffalo that had fled had not deserted the baby; they had gone back for reinforcements! They knew that they weren't strong enough in number and needed help. Surprisingly, the baby water buffalo wobbled to its feet and got swallowed up in the safety of the herd.

I watched in amazement as I listened to the Muskoxes' spiritual analogy of the video. Their point was that it is not God's intention for us to fight our battles alone. God tells us over and over in His Word to pray together and to encourage one another. In order to do that, however, we have to be vulnerable with one another. We have to be real!

Being real was a new concept to me. I had sat in a church pew all of my life. I knew the Christian act. I knew how to wear the mask of perfection. I knew how to smile and pretend that life was wonderful when inside my world was falling apart. I knew how to wear a mask, but being real, I wasn't so sure about that. There was not a single person who knew that I struggled with depression and an eating disorder in addition to low self-esteem. There was not a single person who realized how lonely I truly was because I wore a mask. At the restaurant where I waited tables, I was the comedian. I was wonderful at making my co-workers laugh. None of them knew I struggled with anything. At church and Bible study, I was the pious, Christian girl, quiet and shy but always willing to help. With the few friends I had, I was the listener and the encourager. With my family, I was the obedient daughter, making my weekly call home. Nobody had any clue that I went days without eating or knew that when I did eat, I purged. Nobody had any idea how low my emotions went. I was excellent at pretending to be upbeat all of the time. I knew all about wearing a mask.

Some of the women in this classroom dropped their

masks after the video and became real as they revealed some very private details of their lives to total strangers. I watched in astonishment as the Muskoxes and others in the room began to spiritually fight for them in prayer for nearly an hour. They were the herd of water buffalo coming to the rescue! I was absolutely amazed at this spiritual lesson: that it is not God's intention for us to fight our battles alone. Yet, I wondered if anyone would actually fight for me.

At the prayer conference the next day, I attended Josh's class on praying the Scriptures. Praying God's word and claiming His promises was a new concept to me. I learned so much about prayer at this prayer conference that I had never learned sitting on a pew at church. I shared with Josh and another person that evening in his office about how excited I was to learn to pray the Scriptures. I told him that I wanted to experience the lessons the Muskoxes shared regarding the power of vulnerability and fighting for each other in prayer. He, of course, decided to end our conversation in a group prayer. When it came my turn, I was awkwardly silent as usual until somebody finally closed the prayer. Josh then looked at me and prophesized that one day I would pray aloud and that one day I would lead a Bible study. I laughed at the thought and told him that I was too shy and that I would never do either one. I have since then learned to *never* say that I will *never* do something because God will then make me do just exactly what I don't want to do!

(Living for adventure on top of Mt. Elbert at 14,439 feet)

Chapter 4: The Prayer Partner

When I got home from the prayer conference, I texted Josh and asked him what the title of the book was that the Muskoxes used in their presentation. He gave me one of their phone numbers since he was unsure. At that time, I struggled with social anxiety to the point that it was difficult for me to make a phone call, especially to someone I didn't know. I often wrote a script, even for people that I did know. The problem was that people tended to not follow my script and that left for awkward pauses in the conversation as I struggled to say something. So, I opted for texting Hannah (name changed to protect privacy).

"Hi, this is Tonya from the conference. Josh gave me your number. Can you tell me what the book about prayer promises that your group used is called?"

Some very long minutes passed as I waited for a response. Even texting people caused me anxiety. Finally the response came.

"Hi, the book is called 'Passionate Prayer Promises' by Brenda Walsh. You can buy this on Amazon. Look for the black covered version."

Me: "Thanks so much for the information!"

Hannah: "Sure! Let me know if there is anything else I can help you with!"

Suddenly the idea came to me, so bizarre that I could only assume that it came from God.

"Ask her to pray with you."

I immediately was against that idea. "No way God! Absolutely not!"

This person was beautiful, outgoing, popular, and passionate about prayer. Everything that I wasn't! There was no way that I was going to open myself up for rejection by asking her that. I just knew that she would say no.

"Ask her!"

The thought came stronger.

"ASK HER NOW!"

Finally, I relented, and thought, "Ok, God if You really want me to embarrass myself, but You know that people like that have nothing to do with me!"

I was bullied a lot when I was in school by people exactly like her – the outgoing, popular, church crowd. They were the kind of people who excluded me on a regular basis at church activities. I sat by myself night after night at Youth Group and pretended not to hear while they said negative things about my hair color, freckles, clothing, weight, and personality.

The thought came again:

"Send her a text now and ask her to pray with you!"

I finally typed out the words, “Could you pray with me sometime?” My fingers shook with anxiety as I sent the text.

Long minutes passed with no response.

“See God!” I exclaimed as I paced my kitchen floor. “Why did you set me up for rejection? I knew someone like her wouldn’t bother with someone like me! She is probably laughing her head off at my text! Why did you make me do this?”

After an hour, my phone surprisingly beeped with a text from her. “Sure,” she responded, “I would love to pray with you. I will call you soon.” I stared at my phone in astonishment.

Two weeks passed. The first week, I waited in anticipation for the phone to ring excited with the prospect of someone praying with me and being my Muskox. By the end of the second week, I was glaring at my phone and angry at God for setting me up for rejection.

“I told You she wasn’t going to call me!” I complained to God, disappointed because I desperately wanted what the Muskox group had portrayed. The phone finally rang the third week, and little by little, a phone friendship was formed as Hannah and I became prayer partners. Hannah found it difficult to spiritually fight for me, however, because I had not yet learned how to be vulnerable although she tried very hard to teach me to be real. I loved to go deep spiritually into Scripture with her, but when it came to sharing personal matters, my walls sealed up tight and the mask came on.

Hannah taught me so much about prayer and about God. She encouraged me to pray aloud with her over the phone and offered me a safe, nonjudgmental environment to do just that. I wasn't afraid of her making fun of me like some of the other church people I had known. I'm not sure if she ever knew that I started each conversation the first few months with a script, but even when the script ran out and the long, awkward pauses from me began as I sought words to say, she was always very understanding and encouraging. I did get very annoyed at her constant encouragement to be vulnerable, but, looking back, I now understand how uncomfortable it probably was to talk to someone on a weekly basis who was afraid to let her walls down. She once told me that she did not want a superficial friendship with someone and that that was not worth her time. That hit me hard as I considered her the closest friend that I had ever had, and, out of respect for her and our friendship, I began to slowly crack open the walls that I had built around me.

God used Hannah to teach me vulnerability and to make me comfortable with prayer and with praying aloud with others. He used her to teach me that not all Christian women are two-faced, gossipy, and mean and that some are truly what they appear to be. Hannah knew about my bipolar relationship with God. She knew that sometimes I felt He was love, but that more often, I felt that He was mean. She taught me how to pray the attributes of God and to focus on who He is. To do this, one simply goes through the letters of the alphabet and names an attribute corresponding to the letter. For example:

A: God, You are Amazing and Accept me as I am.

B. God, You are Beautiful.

C. God, You are Compassionate and Caring.

D. God, You are my Deliverer and my Defender.

E. God, You are Excellent.

F. God, You are Forgiving.

G. God, You are full of grace.

And so on. One day, I was driving and feeling very down. So, I began to pray through the attributes of God. But, when I got to the letter “M”, all I could think of was, “God, You are MEAN! You are just plain mean! You torment me with nightmares and insomnia. You made me so ugly with red hair and a zillion freckles that only needy, desperate men want to date me, and they are so desperate that they want to marry me on the first date! The only friend who ever calls me is Hannah, and all she cares about talking about is You! You are so mean!”

I then called Hannah and yelled, “HE IS JUST MEAN! HE IS A TORMENTOR!” I explained to her that I had been praying through the attributes and could not think of a positive attribute for the letter “M”. She paused for a moment and then said, “Let me pray. Father, I thank You for who You are and for all of the wonderful attributes about You. I thank You that You are not mean as Tonya thinks but that instead You are merciful and mighty and that You, above all else, are love.” I nearly hung up the phone on her angry that I couldn’t have a single conservation with her that was not focused on prayer.

Thanks to Hannah and Josh's patience and encouragement, I finally, over a period of time, began to understand that God is not mean, as I once thought, but that He truly is love! As I began to become more confident in who I am in Him, God healed me from the eating disorder and other insecurities. During this time of spiritual growth, God began to tear the walls down that I had built around myself, and I slowly learned to trust and be vulnerable. I also became comfortable praying with her since she had created a safe environment, but I couldn't imagine leading prayer or praying aloud with anyone else. Then, the flood came!

Chapter 5: The Flood

I am an avid hiker and a landscape photographer, so I spent the beginning of September 2013 in the Maroon Bells near Aspen, Colorado, documenting the initial colors of fall. It rained slow and steady for days. Getting tired of the dreary weather, I cut my trip short and headed to my home in the Front Range only to find out that it had been steadily raining for several days there too. I live in a rural area two miles from where the Little Thompson River flows in Larimer County. My neighbors told me that evening, "You should go photograph the rising water of the Little Thompson!" The Little Thompson River is so tiny, a creek really, that I didn't even know it existed near me. I also didn't realize that it flows under four county roads near me that run north to south. Even the bridges over the river are so tiny that most people, myself included, drive right over them without realizing they are there. I am ashamed to admit that I actually had to get directions for where the Little Thompson River was - a mere two miles from my home.

I arrived at the river site in the late evening clutching my camera bag in the pouring rain. It was hard to miss, as many other people had turned out to see this historical occurrence as well. There was almost a festive attitude among the crowd as we looked at the raging, swollen river that was spreading over nearby farmland. Some, like me, were taking pictures with cameras. Others were using cellphones and posing in front of the raging water a few feet below. None of us had any idea of what was coming in the next few hours. Overnight, the water surged causing it to wash out bridges and roadways and everything else in its path. I awoke the morning of September 13 and began to drive north at 6 a.m., having no idea what had happened overnight, only to find that I was stopped by "bridge out" signs every direction I tried to go. I peered in the morning darkness, and all I could see was water everywhere. That tiny little creek that was previously unnoticeable had grown to a raging river that washed out everything in its path including homes and livestock. I later noticed a toilet and a propane tank sailing down the river. This flood was labeled as a widespread historic event, a 100 year flood that devastated fourteen counties in Colorado.

When a natural disaster of historic proportions comes within two miles of your home, it's a wakeup call. I literally stood on four of those bridges over the Little Thompson just hours before they washed away! Life was no longer about me and my own insecurities; it was now about what I could do to help. I searched for a way to get involved and found an opportunity volunteering the next day in a city to the north of me at an evacuation shelter. I was unable to drive north from my home, however, because of the washed out bridges and flooded roads. So, I had to detour about thirty minutes to the south then drive about fifty minutes north to get to Fort Collins, a city that normally only took me thirty minutes to get to. Before I left my home,

I felt God telling me to put on a prayer button.

While I had received the prayer buttons several years prior at the prayer conference that changed my life, I had never worn any of them. They were simple buttons with a picture of a flower engraved with the words, “May I Pray For You?” I am not a flowery kind of girl, however, so I had never put one on. I tried to argue with God.

“I don’t want to wear this!”

He would not let up on the idea. I have learned when things seem bizarre, out of the norm, and are not what I would normally do, God has a plan! So, I put one on, and then forgot about it. I arrived at the evacuation shelter and waited my orders. People were being airlifted in by helicopter from the nearby foothills. We were told to assist them with food, clothing, phones, beds, etc. We were also told not to proselytize and that we could only pray with someone if they asked. I smiled because that was totally okay with me. I wasn’t planning on praying with anyone while there; I was just planning on helping in tangible ways by being Jesus’s hands and feet.

I still struggled with social anxiety at this time. However, my desire to help the flood victims outweighed my own issues. I walked around for a while helping where I was needed. Suddenly, a woman with stricken eyes stopped me.

“Will you?”

I was confused as to what she wanted. I smiled,

“What can I do for you?”

She responded by asking, "Will you?" once again.

I was very confused at this point and wondering if she had a head injury. Once again I asked, "What can I do for you?" with a smile thinking that she might want something simple like a water bottle.

The tears flowed out of her eyes as she asked once more, "Will you pray with me?"

She was reading my prayer button, the button I forgot that I was wearing. I looked at her nervously. I had never led prayer before with anyone except for Hannah.

"Umm, you want me to pray with you?" I questioned.

At her affirming nod, I thought, "Ok God, I don't know what I'm doing here, but here goes". It suddenly was no longer about me. I began to pray aloud with her and soon was joined by four college-aged girls. We knelt on the hard floor of that evacuation shelter, in plain view of everyone, and prayed over this woman and over the other flood victims. I was amazed that not only had I prayed aloud with someone that I didn't even know, but that I had also led prayer. I reflected back to Josh's prophetic words several years prior about praying aloud and leading prayer one day and how I had declared that I would never do either one because I was too shy. God had just made me eat my words!

I knew that volunteering at the evacuation shelter was making a difference; however, I wanted to become more involved in helping. Disaster relief organizations from across the country began rolling in. I soon heard about an opportunity to get involved with disaster relief with Convoy of Hope which is a faith based, non-profit humanitarian organization based in Springfield, Missouri. I made my way to the small Assembly of God church hosting Convoy of Hope the next morning, having no idea what to expect. I didn't know anyone else volunteering with Convoy of Hope; this was a huge step for me with social anxiety. But, the flood had changed me! It was less about me and my insecurities and more about helping those in need. I walked into the church, received a t-shirt and a Hazmat suit along with a respirator, and followed my crew through a National Guard security point into a flood, ravaged area of Longmont, Colorado.

There is no way to put into words the sights and smells of the devastation. The flood had not only brought water into this community but also huge amounts of silt, garbage, and sewage. All along the street, people were bringing out soggy, silt-covered, ruined items and stacking them in huge piles by the curb. Our assignment was a widow in her mid-60's who had a two-story home complete with a finished basement. The flood waters had risen to almost the top of the first story. I entered the home, my rubber boots sinking into the soggy carpet in what was left of the living room. There had been sump pumps running there for several days, but there was still about a foot and a half of water remaining in the basement. This woman was very organized and kept family pictures and other mementos of her life stored in the basement.

I started down the basement stairs gagging at the smell. It was overpowering. Our crew began to make an assembly line hauling item after item up from the basement and outside to the curb for the homeowner to look at and determine if it was worth salvaging or not. After a while, we changed places. I was thankful to now be hauling buckets of items from the front door to the homeowner at the curb versus gagging on the sewage smells in the house through my respirator which really wasn't helping with the overpowering smells. I wasn't paying attention to what the silt covered items were that I was hauling outside to the homeowner. There were some other members of my crew who were outside at the curb with her helping to sort through those items. My job was just to carry it out there. She had been holding up pretty well, laughing and joking with us, and thankful for the help until I hauled out a particular bucket filled with silt-covered pictures. She teared up and began to wail then. Those were her wedding pictures; her husband had recently passed away, just a few months prior to the flood. Those pictures were all she had left of him besides memories.

My crew suddenly put hands on her and began to pray as she shook in anguish. Just like at the evacuation shelter, it suddenly wasn't about me and my fear of being inadequate at public prayer; rather, it was about being there for this woman. I joined in by praying right there at the curb with the others. Our praying for this woman did not bring back what she had lost. But, it let her know that we cared, and more importantly that God cared what she was going through. One only had to take a look around her flood ravaged neighborhood to know that she was not alone in her suffering. But, each person was affected in a different way. For her, losing the last mementos of her husband meant more to her than the damage to her home. Receiving hugs and knowing that others cared meant the world to her. She couldn't understand why we, perfect strangers, were willing to wade through the contaminated, silt filled water in her basement to help her clean up her home. She said over and over that she wanted to put our names in the local newspaper, which we all declined. We weren't there for glory; we were just there to help be Jesus's hands and feet.

I volunteered with Convoy of Hope for the next few months in Longmont and in the nearby cities of Niwot and Lyons until they pulled out. Convoy of Hope was just there to help with immediate needs. When they left, I joined Samaritan's Purse to help with more long-term needs. I learned to rip out drywall a few inches above the water line in homes. I learned to pull out soggy cabinets and used tools I still don't know the name of. Through volunteering with both organizations, I learned to be comfortable walking in a hot Hazmat suit with booties on. I learned safety measures to use when going to the restroom or removing the suits to avoid staph infections which were becoming quite common because of the contaminated water. I learned to work hours on end as a team with people I had just met and not feel socially inferior. I learned to hug complete strangers and became comfortable praying with them.

Just like a physical flood brings about devastation and hurt initially, but eventually results in new growth, God did a spiritual flood in my life. He cleansed me in His power! It was a long process of many years, but eventually new growth became evident in my life. God also used this historic, epic flood to do epic changes in my life. No longer was my life dictated by my own perceived insecurities and inferiorities. Now, I became consumed with the question, "How can I serve others?"

(Cleaning debris from a flooded home)

Chapter 6: The Call to Serve

The prayer conference and the flood were pivotal moments in my life that God used to change me from the inside out. By the end of 2013, most people that I met did not believe me when I told them that I am not outgoing because that is not the person they saw. They didn't see an introvert; they saw an extrovert. They didn't see a shy person; they saw an outgoing person. I still saw myself as all of those things, but that's not who others saw me as anymore.

I became a completely vulnerable, transparent person. I was so amazed at what God had done in me that I couldn't wait to share it with others. Thankfully, the church I attend now is not like this, but some of the churches I attended in the past were filled with people who bought into Satan's lie that Christians don't have troubles. They went to church week after week wearing a mask of perfection. I remember visiting those churches and thinking, "Wow! I don't fit in here. My life is a mess of struggles. Maybe I am too messed up for church!"

Because of those experiences, I resolved to be real and show everyone that I came across that being a Christian does not mean one will not have struggles.

Being a Christian means that when we do struggle and go through hard times that we are not alone because God is always there with us! The truth about God's love is not that He allows bad things to happen, but it is His promise that He will be right there walking beside us when they do happen. I missed that truth for years. Now that I finally understood it, I was eager to share it. Thus, my Facebook ministry began. I began writing so much on a regular basis about what God was doing in my life that the joke among friends became that my posts always said "see more" at the bottom because they were too long to fit in the normal space.

God never intended us to be Christian lone rangers. He tells us over and over in His Word to pray together and encourage one another. We cannot do that unless we are real with one another! I may not have experienced the same struggles as you. But, if we are both honest with each other, we all struggle with something. It may be a struggle with pride or forgiveness, a struggle with depression or anxiety, a struggle with adultery, with stealing, or with poor choices in general. Whatever that struggle may be, Satan wants to keep us in bondage to it. He wants us to fight that battle alone because he knows that when we do, we will become exhausted and pull away from God. That is why it is so important to learn vulnerability because when we are real with one another and ask for prayer, we can spiritually fight for one another.

I began to preach vulnerability over Facebook. I knew what a relief I felt when I was no longer concerned about the world knowing my secrets. As Pastor Josh says, "We are only as sick as our secrets". Satan tries to keep us in bondage by asking, "What will people think of you if they only knew?" I am here to tell you when you drop your pride and become real, it is one of the most freeing emotions you will ever feel! You are no longer held in bondage, captive to Satan's lies. You are free in Christ! Also, by sharing your story, you will help someone else who thinks that they are the only one struggling with something. As Priscilla Shirer says, "Our messes become our greatest message!" *

In fall of 2014, I felt God's leading to start a Bible study. Me – not only start a Bible study but lead it! I did my usual Moses thing with God.

"God, I'm too shy; I can't do this. Isn't there someone else?"

Nope, God wanted me! God worked out all of the details, and I soon found myself leading a study by Priscilla Shirer. The irony of the topic of the study was not lost on me. It was about Jonah and presented the question of "What is God calling you to do that you are trying to avoid?" Ouch! Pretty much everything God called me to do, I tried to avoid and made up an excuse for. I knew in my heart that God was calling me to the ministry in some form, but I wanted to avoid it. God spoke to me during that study and pretty soon I found myself not only leading that one once a week but also leading another study once a month. Once again, I remembered sitting in Josh's office those many years ago and declaring that not only would I never pray aloud or lead prayer but that I would also never lead a Bible study. I am learning to stop telling God that I am never going to do stuff because He ends up making me do it eventually!

In addition to the Bible studies that I was leading, I

began volunteering at Christian humanitarian events interacting with hundreds of people. Me, the shy, socially insecure person, interacting with hundreds of people that I had never met! I never once saw that coming!

I have felt God's call to write this book and not only share the God moments and analogies that He has given me, but also to share my story. My story is not necessarily unique in any way, but I pray that by reading it you are able to see just how much God can change a person. I am not the person I used to be. In fact, I don't even recognize myself anymore! That is how much God has changed me! He has given me confidence instead of fear and doubt. He has given me strength instead of weakness. He has shown me what relationship is all about. He has proven that He is not just words on a page, but that He is real and that He truly cares. He has proven that He is not mean as I once thought but instead is loving.

God has taught me to be vulnerable and has used that transparency in my life to encourage others. I am a living testimony of what God can do in a person's life. But, the thing is, we have to allow Him to work in our lives. He is a gentleman. He will not force His way in. For years, my life was spiritually stagnant. Yet, even during those stagnant years, God had not forgotten me. He used people like Hannah, Josh, and my mom to plant spiritual seeds that would eventually sprout. In my case, it took a very long time for those spiritual seeds to sprout, but that also gives hope to all of us for when we sow seeds in others, sometimes we don't get to see those sprout right away. However, God declares that His Word will not return void (Isaiah 55:10-11

NIV).

As you read the next sections of this book, I pray that you will be inspired and encouraged as to just how big God truly is!

*("Life Interrupted" by Priscilla Shirer pg. 38)

Part 2: God Moments

Chapter 1: Stranded in Kentucky

I was first introduced to caving at Jewel Cave National Monument in the Black Hills of South Dakota. A park ranger there showed me a small concrete box and told me that only those who can fit through that box can experience the adventure of a lifetime. I was intrigued and signed up for their spelunking tour after meeting the box requirements. Having no background in bouldering techniques, I was terrified for most of the tour as we chimneyed and chambered over open pits with no rope, but I became hooked on caving afterwards. I later learned that Jewel Cave's program is the hardest in the country!

I began to search out other caving courses and found an intriguing all day one at Mammoth Cave in Kentucky. I arrived there a few days before my scheduled class and began to explore the nearby trails. Near the park, I saw a series of small, homemade signs advertising canoe rentals on the Green River. I loved to canoe, so I followed the wooden signs to a small, run-down shack. There were three steps leading from the ground to the porch of the shack. Two of those steps were rotted! I walked inside and saw a lone man fanning himself in the summer heat.

"What kin I do fer ya?" he drawled.

Undeterred by the look of the shack, I replied, "I would like to rent a canoe please".

The man slowly looked me up and down as he shook his head and declared, "I can't rent ya a canoe."

Confused, I looked around. Near the rotted steps of the porch were several empty canoes.

"Why not?"

The man looked at me as if I were from another planet. "Cuz yer a woman!"

Since this was the year 2001 and not the late 1800's, I was very confused.

"What does that have to do with me renting a canoe?"

The man explained, "Women can't handle no canoe by themselves".

I was starting to feel offended. The Green River looked peaceful. I didn't even see any rapids on it. I couldn't see any problem with handling the canoe on my own, so I decided to get forceful.

"Look this is a canoe rental shop. I have cash to rent a canoe. I will take responsibility for myself."

The man finally yielded and allowed me to rent a canoe all the while loudly expressing how much he disagreed with doing so. He explained where the pick-up point would be down the river, and we agreed on a time frame.

I hopped in the canoe smiling as I set out on the Green River. I had won that battle! It was a beautiful sunny, hot day, and I longed to take a dip in the murky waters below. First, I decided to explore for a while. I found some cave openings and paddled my way inside as far back as I could see. Not having a headlamp with me, I backed the canoe out and continued downriver. The scenery was amazing, and I was having a great time until I hit a small rapid which bumped me into a large beaver dam of driftwood. In doing so, I disturbed a nest of water moccasins who quickly began trying to slither into my canoe. I hit them with my paddles as I screamed a scream that could wake up the dead. I imagine that man in the canoe rental shack was probably smiling to himself thinking, “Yep, women can’t handle canoes!”

I whacked at the snakes with my paddles until they finally gave up on my canoe and slid into the water. There was no way I was going swimming in that river now! I pushed myself off the dam and continued on my way to the pick-up point. The second half of my river journey was nowhere near as fun as the first half as I was now afraid of snakes coming in my canoe! Reaching the pick-up point with no more problems, I dragged the canoe up on the shore and waited for the man to arrive. He seemed impressed that I had handled the canoe just fine. I didn’t share my snake story with him though!

Afterwards, I began to drive around the Kentucky hills along the backroads and found a small sign next to a dirt road stating “Historic Schoolhouse this way”. I am fascinated by history and old structures, so I angled my rental truck down the dirt road which began as a series of sharp descents. After driving about five miles with no schoolhouse in sight and with each descent getting steeper, I decided to turn around. The sign hadn't stated how far away that old schoolhouse was, and I didn't want to waste all afternoon driving around looking for it. Plus, the road was beginning to make me a little nervous. One side of the road dropped into a ravine while the other side of the road flanked the mountainside.

I turned the rental truck around at the base of the last steep descent and pushed the gas to drive up the hill. To my surprise, the truck tires spun, and the vehicle slid toward the ravine. I had never experienced something like that before, so I tried pushing the gas again. The tires spun and pushed me closer to the edge. Starting to get scared, I quickly got out of the truck and placed the floor mats underneath the tires for traction with the same result. The tires just spun and slid. I frantically began pulling on the nearby kudzu and vegetation, stuffing whatever I could tear off underneath the tires. Still, the tires spun over and over. I was stuck on a backwoods Kentucky mountain road, and not a single person knew where I was since driving down this road had been a spontaneous decision.

Realizing that I wasn't going to be able to drive that truck up the hill and not knowing where the road would come out or if it dead ended somewhere, I began to hike back toward the main road. Since I had flown into Kentucky, I didn't have my usual hiking gear with me. No knife. No mace. I pride myself on being tough and on being able to handle situations, but thinking of the financial repercussions of my stuck rental truck had me in tears. My legs and arms were covered in dirt and scratches from frantically grabbing at the nearby vegetation to place underneath my tires. I knew I had driven about five miles from the main road, and I began to plod along. Thankfully, I had my GPS and a water bottle with me. I remembered that there had been a house next to the main road at the turnoff for the historic school. As I hiked along, I rehearsed my plea for help to the homeowners.

I finally arrived at the house I remembered and knocked on the door. No answer. I wasn't sure if nobody was home or if whoever was there was scared of the sight of me, tear marks streaking down my face, and arms and legs covered in dust. I sat on the ground in a panic. I had a cell phone, but who would I call in Kentucky, and besides, I didn't even know where I was. I pulled out my phone to see if I even had service. Nope, out of range! Tears streaming down my face at this point, I made my way to the main road and stuck up my thumb just as I heard the sound of a vehicle approaching. To my surprise, the driver slowed and then stopped in front of me. It was a beat up old truck driven by an old man who had what appeared to be only four teeth.

"What's yer problem?" he asked.

Stuttering, I replied. "I d-d-d rove my truck d-d-down that road t-t-towards the schoolhouse, and and and I c-c-can't get it back up. It's s-s-stuck!"

"They need to put a sign on that road, " the man said. "People always getting stuck in there. I gots me a tow hitch. Hop in, and let's see if I can get ya out." He leaned over and opened the passenger side door.

I looked at the man with his four teeth then down at what was once a bench seat but now had only springs sticking up. I had to make an instant decision. Stay here and thumb someone else down. Or, go with this creepy stranger back down that lonesome road where nobody knows where I am. Knowing that I had to try to get my rental truck out of there somehow and not knowing when anyone else would happen to drive along the main road, I got in, but sat as close to the door as possible. As he began making his way down the dirt road towards my abandoned truck, scenes from the many horror movies I had watched in my youth filled my mind. Single words and phrases began playing in my head like warnings: stranger, backwoods, no knife, no mace, nobody knows where I am, truck stuck.

Having no idea what was going on in my head, the man kept up a lively chatter as he maneuvered the sharp, winding roads.

"Yes ma'am. People get stuck back here all the time looking for that there schoolhouse. I got me that tow chain just to pull them out. Good thing I came along though. These roads ain't traveled much." He continued chattering as I braced myself to keep from bouncing on the spring exposed seat. We finally arrived at the top of the hill that my truck was stuck on the bottom of.

"Oh no, I was afraid of that!" he exclaimed. "That hill is the worst! I'm not sure if my truck can get back up that one with yours. Let me walk down and see what I can do first." He told me to stay at the top of the hill by his truck as I handed him my rental's keys. He carefully walked down the steep hill and climbed into my rental truck. I watched the truck do the same thing with him that it had done with me. The more the gas was pushed, the more the tires spun and slid toward the ravine. He attempted the same thing a few times then pressed hard on the gas. It finally started moving upwards a little but slid dangerously close to the side. I watched in horror as he kept gunning it; the truck finally gained momentum and climbed to the top of the hill next to me. Shaking in relief that the man didn't slide into the ravine while trying to help me, I thanked him profusely.

"You just have to accelerate hard on this," he explained then asked me to lead the way out just in case I had any more problems. Mile after mile I drove until I reached the intersection with the main road once again. The man was still behind me in his truck as he had been for the past five miles watching to see if I got stuck again. Putting the truck in park, I reached into my purse and began to dig out my wallet planning on giving the man a twenty dollar bill for his help, but when I opened my door, he was gone.

You might be thinking as you read this that there has to be a plausible explanation. After all, trucks don't just disappear in seconds when you are blocking the road while you dig in your purse for cash. I am a very analytical person, and believe me I searched around for credible answers. First of all, that truck was very noisy. It probably hadn't seen a muffler in years! If he had driven off into the grass around me, I would have heard it. Secondly, even that was not possible because there was a small drainage ditch on each side of the dirt road at that point.

Where did he go? Where did he come from? I pondered those very questions as I made my way back to the ferry across the Green River. How did his truck just vanish from sight? How was he behind me one minute at the intersection with the main road, then gone the next? There wasn't enough room for him to have gone around me. Chills filled me as I made the only conclusion possible. God had sent an angel to help me! I had not asked for help from God; I was too busy trying to handle the problem with the stuck truck on my own. But, God in His infinite wisdom, knowledge, and love not only knew that I needed help but sent me the most unlikely form of help –a beat up old truck, a semi toothless man with only four teeth, and a bench seat covered in springs.

What are you struggling with today? What are you stuck in? What are you trying to handle on your own? God sees your tears, and He knows your needs. He states in Matthew 10:31 that you are valuable to Him and asks you not to worry because He sees your needs and will provide (Matthew 6:25).

"So don't worry about these things, saying, 'What will we eat? What will we drink? What will we wear?' Your Heavenly Father already knows all your needs." (Matthew 6:31-31).

(Kentucky road lined with kudzu and vegetation)

Chapter 2: Alone in the Wilderness

I love to hike in the wilderness in particular the desert canyons of the Southwest. These canyons aren't quite desert because there are springs of water and hidden pools hidden amongst the barren landscape. Even though it breaks all of the rules of hiking and canyoneering, I often go alone. Without distractions of human conversation, I can fully experience solitude in the wild and appreciate how small I am and how big God is when standing in the bottom of a canyon looking at the towering walls around me.

In late April of 2014, I set off on a forty mile journey into the isolated wilderness of a remote section of Utah. Canyoneering involves more than just hiking, bouldering, and route-finding. One has to be aware of the dangers of patches of quicksand and flash floods as well as rattlesnakes and scorpions. There are few trails and few encounters with other humans. In fact, one can go days without seeing another person in the remote wilderness areas of Utah. That is why I love it! I don't set off naively on these journeys, however. Given the fact that there are few visitors to these remote areas, I know that means that I cannot count on outside help for problems. It is just me and God.

I was having a wonderful time on this journey witnessing the beauty of God's creation in small arches, rock formations, and in the desert itself when I made the ultimate mistake. I over estimated my abilities. In my wanderings, I arrived at the base of a thirty foot pour-off which, had it been raining, would have been a beautiful waterfall. This pour-off stood between me and my destination which I was very close to. I am a photographer, and I had a beautiful, rarely seen, arch in mind to photograph. I studied the pour-off; the left side appeared extremely difficult to ascend. I chose the right side and began slowly making my way up placing my fingers in small holds in the clefts of the rock. I was having a very difficult time getting handholds and footholds by the time I got to about the midway point, but I just kept my eyes focused on the top.

I finally reached the top of the pour-off and began to hike toward the nearby arch. This area was an island of rock surrounded by drop-offs on all sides. The only accessible way to get up there freestyle, in my opinion, was the way I had come. I dropped my pack on the ground, pulled out my camera equipment, and photographed the amazingly, beautiful arch. It was an awesome experience being the only one up there! I admit that I am sort of a free spirit, and I had no problem relieving myself up there. After all, I was the only person for miles and miles. Who would see me?

After lunch and a rest break, I began to load up my gear for the hike down. There were some storm clouds moving in, and I did not want to be exposed up there. I happily made my way back to the thirty foot pour-off then stopped mouth gaping.

"Wait! I didn't climb up this, did I? I can't climb

down that!"

I realized then that I had made the tragic mistake that so many others have in Utah; it is much easier to climb up than it is to climb down. Legs shaking, I made my way to the edge and sat down studying possible routes. I glanced at the wall to the right of me; this was the side that I had deemed too dangerous to go up. It looked just as dangerous to descend. I was going to have to go back down the same route I had gone up; only now this route looked extremely difficult and dangerous.

I now carry a two-way satellite communicator that I can use to get in touch with Search and Rescue for jams such as this. However, at that time, I did not carry one. I had refused to buy one because I felt they were too expensive. I thought that my system of leaving my hiking information with a friend and telling her that I would check in within a week was good enough. After all, I was an experienced hiker. What could go wrong? I never imagined myself stuck at the top of a pour-off in the remote wilderness of Utah. Suddenly the isolation that I had previously craved and enjoyed seemed suffocating. I wanted people around; I wanted help. I did not want to try to descend this alone.

Nevertheless, alone is exactly what I was. Storm clouds were rolling in; there was a strong possibility of lightning strikes in this exposed area. Plus, if it started raining, I would not be able to descend the pour-off for quite some time. Slickrock is named slickrock for a reason! It is easy to walk on when dry, but when wet, think slip and slide. No traction! I nervously looked down the pour-off again. I am much more confident climbing up something than down. This looked impossible! In canyoneering terms, I was cliffed-out!

I debated my options. Stay up here and wait four more days for my friend Diane to notice that I have not checked in. Then, wait while a Search and Rescue unit got organized and tried to figure out where, on my week's itinerary that I had left with Diane, I could be. I was on a forty mile journey in the remote wilderness! They would have a hard time narrowing down where to search. Wait or go? The words echoed in my head. Should I stay, or should I go? The clouds were getting darker; I made my decision. I would try to descend.

I made my way to the edge once more then prayed the words to Matt Maher's song, "Lord, I Need You":

"Lord, I need You, oh I need You.

Every hour I need You.

My one defense, my righteousness,

Oh, God, I need You."

I got to the stanza that says "When I cannot stand, I'll fall on You. Jesus, You're my hope and stay" and began to cry. Yes, I physically was alone, but as a Christian, I knew that I am never truly alone because God is always with me. He is my hope and my anchor. I prayed for God's protection. I prayed that He would send someone to spot me. I knew that was unlikely. After all, I had happily relieved myself at the top because there was nobody there. It's not like people are just going to appear out of nowhere. Yet, I prayed anyway for God to send me help or show me a better route down. Then, I waited.

Waiting is not my strong point. I'm not good at it. I waited five minutes for God to answer my prayer then decided to take some action when He apparently didn't. I tentatively began to lower myself over the side, realizing as I did that it was going to be very hard to get handholds initially. Scared, I pulled myself back up and began to shake all over at this dilemma. I worked up the courage to try again and started inching my way back over to the edge when I heard a voice behind me ask, "Are you okay?" In shock, I turned around. There was a man and a woman behind me. Behind me! As in nobody was there a few minutes ago on that small island of rock and now suddenly two people were standing behind me! Whoa! My first thought was, "Where were they? Did they see me pee up here?" I then noticed that neither of them had packs on. That was odd! No packs and no water supply in the desert heat. Weird!

I didn't spend time analyzing their lack of preparedness, however, considering that here I was stuck at the top of a pour-off. Who was I to judge? I replied, "I'm just trying to work up the courage to descend this. It looks really intimidating."

The man nodded his head and asked, "Do you want us to spot you?" I thankfully nodded my head in an affirmative "yes". They began making their way down the right side; the side that I had ruled out because it appeared more difficult than the side I had ascended. The man braced himself midway and turned around to spot me. As he showed me where to place my hands and shaking feet, I descended quite easily with no problems. Having a spotter made all the difference! It wasn't that I didn't have the ability to descend; the problem was that I had let fear overcome me once I saw from the top just how steep the pour-off looked. Fear is a climber's worst enemy! This couple's guidance made all the difference for me and gave me the confidence I needed to descend.

Finally putting my feet on the warm, desert sand below the pour-off, I knelt and prayed, "Thank You, Thank You, Thank You God!" in gratitude. When I looked up to thank the couple for their assistance, to my surprise, they were gone. Where did they go? How had they disappeared that quickly? Could it be that for the second time in my life God had sent an angel in disguise to help me? Was that why they didn't have any backpacks or water bottles in the desert heat? Does God really love me that much that He had just bailed me out of yet another jam I had gotten myself into?

Maybe you are in a wilderness, spiritually speaking, and right now you are staring in fear at the pour-off in your life. You might be facing any number of problems and thinking, "This is impossible! I can't do this alone! This is too intimidating, too overwhelming. The problem is too big!" Maybe you are having doubts about your faith or struggling with anxiety and fear. If pour-offs in your life are occupying your heart and your mind more than your faith is, I want to remind you that the same power that raised Jesus from the dead can transform your life! He can remove the fear and doubt and give you courage and strength as you grow in faith and learn to rely on Him!

As you begin to truly believe that you can do all things through Christ who strengthens you (Philippians 4:13), you will develop confidence in God instead of in yourself and in your own abilities. As you begin to truly understand just how deep, how long, how wide, and how high God's love is for you (Ephesians 3:18), you will grow to understand that absolutely nothing is impossible with God (Luke 1:37)! People appearing out of nowhere in the wilderness to help you is absolutely no problem for God to make happen! God makes the impossible possible!

Pray God's promises over your life and believe them. Believe that God truly cares about you! Call on Him and pray, "Lord, I need You! I can't do this on my own! I need You!" You do not have to stay in the wilderness, and you do not have to face spiritual pour-offs on your own. There is power in prayer and in calling on the name of Jesus Christ!

God knows everything about you. He knows when you sit down and when you stand up (Psalm 139: 1-2). He knows the number of hairs on your head (Luke 12:7). And, He knows what you are going through. He knows what you are struggling with. He knows what you are afraid of and what you are discouraged about. He knows, and He cares. God cares for you! Whatever the spiritual pour-off may be that you are facing right now, believe that nothing, absolutely nothing, is impossible with God! No matter how isolated this wilderness may seem, you are never truly alone for God is always with you!

"For nothing is impossible with God." (Luke 1:37)

(self-timer picture at the top of a pour-off

Chapter 3: Trick Riding

Let me start out by saying that I am not a cowgirl. Oh, I can dress the part in my cute straw hat coupled with jeans and boots, but dressing like a cowgirl does not in any way make me a cowgirl any more than going to church makes one a Christian. With my Southern accent, I can easily talk like a cowgirl, but talking like one doesn't actually make me one either. I can look the part, and I can talk the talk, but when it comes down to it, I have no idea what being a real cowgirl is all about.

I learned that lesson the hard way when I was eighteen. I would roll my windows down and drive through the streets of my rural town with my radio blasting out country music while letting out a loud "Yeehaw"! Yep, I was a cowgirl all right! I loved horses; they were beautiful to look at. I read every book I could get my hands on about horses and went to every rodeo event in the nearby area. I talked the talk and convinced my co-workers that I was an expert rider. In fact, I even convinced myself though I had never spent more than a couple of hours on one in my entire life. After all, how hard could it be to sit on a horse and go for a ride? I had read all about it. How hard could it be to put into practice what I had learned?

One day, some co-workers and I decided to visit a nearby park that had horse rentals for the trails. My co-workers were newbies and had no idea what they were doing. I smiled as I knowledgably explained to them that horses sometimes puff out their stomachs while the saddle is being placed on them which is why it is important to check the saddle before climbing on. I kept up nonstop chatter as I explained the wrangler's every move to them as he saddled the horses for us. I had read so much about horseback riding. I thought I knew everything there was to know.

Finally, we hoisted ourselves into the saddles. My co-workers were visibly nervous, but not me. With a huge smile, I lightly tapped my feet into the horse's side to get it to speed up. Riding was a piece of cake just like the books I had read. I looked behind me in triumph. My co-workers were eating my dust! Then, something strange happened that I wasn't prepared for. My saddle began slipping to the side. As I began to slip to the side of the horse's body with it, I began to panic. This wasn't in my books! What was happening? I realized then that while I was showing off being Miss Know-It-All, I distracted the wrangler who apparently forgot to check my saddle's cinching. My saddle was too loose!

My co-workers back behind me were cheering. "Yay! Way to go!" They thought that I was doing tricks for them. They had no idea that I was in full panic mode trying not to fall off the horse. At this point, the saddle, with me in it, had slipped halfway down the side of the horse. I was trying in vain to pull on the reins to slow the horse down, but the odd feel of my weight and the saddle's placement must have spooked him. He picked up his speed. My friends cheered loudly as we ran in circles, me hanging on sideways like a circus performer. This was great entertainment for them! I began to scream as I felt myself slipping more and more until finally I couldn't hang on any longer. As I fell, one foot remained caught in the stirrup. The panicked horse continued to run as I was dragged on the ground near its trampling hooves, dangling by one foot in the stirrup.

Finally realizing that I wasn't putting on a show and that I was truly in danger due to my terrified screams, my co-workers got the wrangler's attention. He trotted over, grabbed the reins somehow, and calmed the horse down as someone removed my foot from the stirrup. Laying on the ground, breathing rapidly, tears streaming, and covered in blood, I visibly shook at the thought of those hooves nearly trampling me. My know-it-all attitude had almost cost me my life!

God protected me during that episode. I walked away with only some nasty bruises and cuts. It could have been much, much worse. In fact, a few years later, I got bucked off a horse so bad that I had reverse whiplash which hurt for quite some time. I would like to say that this episode taught me to respect a horse's power, but it actually took me several years to learn that lesson. Looking back, however, the one thing I learned from my day of "trick riding" is that it takes more than dressing like a cowgirl and talking like a cowgirl to be a true cowgirl. It takes more than just reading about being a cowgirl to actually become one.

The same is true in our spiritual lives. We can talk the talk as a Christian. We can act super religious and avoid certain foods and worship on certain days. We can dress as piously as possible. We can carry our

Bibles with us everywhere we go and look religious. We can go to church whenever the doors are open and lead Bible studies or sing in the praise and worship band. We can read inspirational books on what being a Christian is all about. We can quote numerous Bible verses and make sure that the person sitting in the pew next to us can see our highlighted texts in our Bibles so that they know just how religious we are. We can put bumper stickers on our vehicles with religious symbols. We can wear a cross necklace around our necks and WWJD bracelets on our wrists so that people can identify us as Christians. We can pray the most elaborate prayers. We can post quotes and Scripture on social media every day. We can look the part and act the part of a good religious Christian, but unless we truly have a relationship with Jesus Christ, it is all meaningless. It is like me actually believing that I was a cowgirl just because I had read how to be one and dressed and talked like one.

God says in Isaiah 29:13, *"These people say they are Mine. They honor me with their lips, but their hearts are far from Me. And their worship of Me is nothing but man-made rules learned by rote."*

God wants us to worship Him with a sincere heart. Since He already knows everything about us, He can't be deceived. He knows what our motives are. He knows if we are sincerely seeking to serve Him, or if we are seeking to glorify ourselves. God wants our love over tradition. God wants a true relationship with us. It doesn't matter if we can talk the Christian talk or dress the part. It doesn't matter if we have read everything there is to know about being a Christian. Knowledge of God is not the same as knowing God! God is so much more than just words on a page or religious traditions! You can read all about God. Unless you truly know God and have a relationship with Him, you are just sliding off a horse on a loose saddle.

Knowing God is a mixture of heart and mind.

"Trust in the Lord with all your heart; do not depend on your own understanding. Seek His will in all you do, and He will show you which path to take. Don't be impressed with your own wisdom." (Proverbs 3:5-7)

Do you truly know God and not just about God? Or, are you in your own wisdom, going through meaningless, religious motions? When we truly know someone and care about them, we make a point to learn their likes and dislikes. Do you know what is important to God? Do you know what He likes and what He dislikes? In Hosea 6:6, God states,

"I want you to show love, not offer sacrifices. I want you to know Me more than I want burnt offerings."

God doesn't want us just going through the motions. He wants our hearts!

Have you given God your heart?

"These people honor Me with their lips, but their hearts are far from Me. Their worship is a farce." (Mark7:6-7)

(Standing in an old mine building)

Chapter 4: Herding Cattle in the Canyon

A few years ago, I set out for a five day hiking adventure in the vast BLM lands of the Grand Gulch in Utah in search of ancient Anasazi ruins to photograph. I am enthralled with the mysterious disappearance of that entire culture of people and enjoy finding remote ruins and the drawings they left behind in the form of pictographs and petroglyphs. The great thing about this area is that there are few trails and few people. When I find ancient red and white handprints decorating an alcove wall, I feel a connection with these past people who seem to be saying through the prints they left behind, "I was real. Don't forget me. I mattered." I love to find tiny shriveled up corn cobs, signs of their meager diet, and pottery fragments as I imagine the individual stories of these people.

On this particular trip, I was looking to explore ancient ruins and photograph relics. The canyon that I was exploring was full of arroyos, small washes, springs, and lots of alcoves. It was a fairly lush canyon as far as Utah goes with a fair amount of vegetation. As I plodded across the sand and dirt, I noticed no trace of anyone who might have passed before me. Perhaps the wind had obliterated their footprints, or maybe a significant period of time had passed since the last person visited this remote area. Leaving "breadcrumbs" on my GPS so that I could find my way back, I happily hiked along enjoying the peaceful silence in the canyon. I climbed to the top of an arroyo, descended the other side, entered a narrow canyon, rounded a curve where I began to see and feel the shade of some cottonwood trees, and suddenly came face to face with twenty-five cattle that were enjoying the shade of the trees and a nearby alcove. I don't know who was more surprised – me or the cattle!

One of the cattle in particular, I dubbed her "Big Mama", resented my intrusion and began to do what I can only describe as a snorting bellow, definitely not a traditional "moo", while pawing at the ground and glaring at me. The other cattle followed her lead and began to "moo" but remained lying down. The cattle were obviously feeling nervous at my intrusion, and I was definitely feeling nervous trapped in a narrow canyon with them. I attempted to calm them down by speaking to them in a sing-song voice as one would an aggressive dog. "It's okay. I'm not going to hurt you. I just need to pass you."

All of the cattle continued to rest in the shade except for Big Mama. She gave me some very nasty looks as she bellowed, snorted, and pawed the ground with her hooves. There were about seven calves in the herd of twenty-five. I wondered if Big Mama was behaving that way because she felt that I was a threat to the calves. I once again tried to calm the cattle down in a sing-song voice. "Good cattle. It's okay. I'm not going to hurt you." Big Mama seemed to become angrier at that.

I admit that I know very little about cattle, but I

love to attend rodeos. I suddenly remembered from my years of watching rodeos that something about the color red irritates bulls. Maybe the same is true for cattle. I happen to have bright red hair, and I was wearing a red and orange bandanna tied around my head. I quickly put my white climbing helmet on thinking that might calm Big Mama down. I was feeling a little frightened at this point knowing just how fast these animals can run and fearing that I might get trampled in this narrow canyon bed if they stampeded since there was really nowhere to go for safety. I didn't think that I could boulder my way up the sheer walls at that point.

As an avid hiker, I am prepared for a lot of things that could go wrong in the wilderness. I carry a snake bite kit and a first aid kit. I also carry a huge canister of bear mace which will temporarily blind a bear; thankfully, I have never had to use it. However, one can of bear mace versus twenty-five angry cattle was not good odds! Since I had not noticed any signs of recent visitors to this area, my chances of getting help were not good if I got trampled or mauled. Lack of immediate help is definitely a downside to solo hiking and canyoneering. My options were to back away slowly and return the way I came or find a way to proceed. Since I really wanted to discover new ruins that I had not previously explored, adventure won. I just needed to find a way around the cattle obstacle.

Just then God brought to mind some phrases I had heard at a cowboy church that I occasionally visit: "Move along now! Get on outta here!" I very timidly spoke these phrases to Big Mama, and to my surprise, instantly as a body of one, all of the cattle rose and began to move away from me. Mouth agape, I stood there in amazement that twenty-five cattle, including Big Mama who obviously disliked me, moved instantly at the sound of my timid command! Big Mama bellowed her displeasure at me, but she moved along with the rest. I was totally in shock that they actually moved. I mean I am 5'1 and weigh 110 pounds. I am not sure what cattle weigh, but it is definitely a lot more than I do! Why would they have listened to anything I said?

I continued picking my way through the vegetation in the canyon bed without seeing the cattle for about an hour until I came to another shady alcove. The cattle were once again lying in the shade and startled by my approach. The “mooing” started up immediately. Feeling more confident after that morning's experience, I commanded in a bold voice, “Move along now! Get on outta here!” Once again, instantly, as a body of one, the animals all rose and began to walk! I was filled with amazement that a herd of cattle listened to me for the second time! The only reason that I could figure is that maybe those are commands the cattle were trained to obey. Whatever the reason, this was pretty cool!

The same experience happened a third time that day further up the canyon in yet another shady area. Once again, I issued the command, “Move along now! Get on outta here!” Once again, they obeyed. “How cool is it,” I thought, “that these cattle obey me when compared to them, I am just a twig!” The cattle mooed their displeasure at having to leave their shady alcove as they plodded along. I continued to command, “Hush now! Move along! Get on outta here!” four more times in the next fifteen minutes as they were headed the same direction I was.

I finally got to a spot where I could see a huge ruin above me and began to scramble my way up. As I scrambled above them, the cattle continued mooing at me. I was focused on my route up and not on them, so by rote at this point, I continued to command, "Get on outta here!" They continued complaining loudly, and I finally looked down at them and noticed that I had somehow herded them into a dead end. The canyon bed in front of them closed off into high, impassible walls! No wonder they were complaining so mightily at me! I laughed as I continued to scramble up toward the ruin, still in amazement that the cattle obeyed me. Hundreds of pounds versus one hundred ten pounds! Twenty-five cattle versus one woman! It didn't make sense!

God gave me a spiritual lesson to share out of this herding experience. The only reason that I could think of for those cattle moving was that God gave me the right words to say by reminding me of phrases I had heard at the cowboy church and at rodeo events. Politely asking them to "Please move", talking to them in a sing-song voice, explaining to them that I was not going to hurt them – none of that worked. Only the phrases "Move along now! Get on outta here!" worked. Those were the only commands the cattle responded to. The only reason they moved is because I said the right commands. They didn't move because they were intimidated by me, although I must have looked quite a sight in my climbing helmet! The cattle responded to what I can only guess are the commands they had been trained to respond to.

As Christians, we know that our battles are not against human opponents but rather against invisible forces of darkness (Ephesians 6:12). Satan knows where our weakest point is, and that is exactly where he tries to attack. He attacks us when we are alone by reminding us of our mistakes, failures, shames, insecurities, etc. He does everything he can to bring us down. But, we do not have to be afraid or intimidated because if we belong to Jesus, if we have confessed our sins and accepted Jesus as our Lord and Savior, we have the key command to invoke to make Satan and his demons leave us alone! They have no power over us because we can stand behind the powerful name of Jesus whom even demons obey! (Luke 10:17) Jesus is our strength, our shield, and our defender! When you are facing a spiritual battle, when the forces of darkness are trying to bring you down, lower your pride, submit to God, and invoke the name of Jesus Christ! Command Satan to leave you alone in the name of Jesus, and just like those cattle, he will obey! (James 4:7) Not because we intimidate him, not because of who we are, but he will obey because there is power in the name of Jesus Christ!

In the past, when Satan tried to get me down, I futilely tried to fight my way through the battles alone. I fought my way through sleepless nights when Satan condemned me for my failures and for not being good enough. I fought my way through depression and eating disorders. I fought my way through low self-worth. I fought my way through those times of extreme loneliness when Satan pestered me to no end that my phone never rang because nobody cared about me. I fought and fought! The thing about fighting battles alone though is that it is extremely exhausting! We can only fight battles alone out of sheer will for so long; eventually, we no longer have the strength to fight.

I began to believe every critical, condemning word he whispered in my ear until one day, thanks to my prayer partner Hannah, I learned to let Jesus do my fighting for me! The next time Satan began to whisper condemning thoughts to me, I invoked the name of Jesus Christ and commanded Satan to leave me alone in the name of Jesus Christ. And, he did! Not because I'm tougher than him, not because I'm bigger than him, not because he was scared of me in any way, but simply because I said the right command! He left me alone because there is power in the name of Jesus Christ! (Philippians 2:10).

If you are struggling today, if you are feeling down, depressed, alone, insecure, or not good enough, you are under spiritual attack! If you know Jesus Christ as your personal Lord and Savior, you have the key command to rebuke the invisible forces of darkness in Jesus's name! Don't waste time trying to futilely plead with Satan to leave you alone like I wasted time pleading with the cattle. Stand behind Jesus as your strength, your shield, your refuge, and your place of safety (Psalm 91)! Command Satan in the name of Jesus Christ to flee from your home, to flee from your life, to flee from your marriage, to flee from your family's life! The Lord says, "I will rescue those who love Me. I will protect those who trust in My name. When they call on Me, I will answer. I will be with them in trouble. I will rescue and honor them. I will reward them with a long life and give them My salvation." (Psalm 91: 14-16)

"So humble yourselves before God. Resist the devil, and he will flee from you." (James 4:7)

(ancient ruin in a remote area of Utah)

Chapter 5: Saying No to Kings

In addition to being a photographer, I am also an inspirational speaker. I share a presentation entitled "Step into the Light" at numerous church events as a way to point people to Jesus through spiritual analogies based on my caving experiences. Public speaking is just one more thing that I never imagined myself doing. As I previously mentioned, I was shy, withdrawn, and insecure. Those are not characteristics of an inspirational speaker! However, I have learned through the years to stop saying "no" to opportunities based on fear unless I truly have a good reason to turn down the opportunity. When the opportunity to speak first presented itself, I did the Moses thing though. "God, you know I'm too shy. I can't get up there and speak in front of all those people. Can't you send someone else?"

God apparently wanted me. I stopped behaving like Jonah trying to run from what God wanted me to do. Just like Jonah, however, I didn't exactly happily embrace it either. I dreaded my speaking engagements. I was incredibly nervous each time I spoke and talked so fast during my speeches that people actually had to ask me to slow down! Just like everything else in my life, God used this opportunity to grow me. I slowly began to develop more confidence as a speaker and actually looked forward to sharing my presentations until one day I was asked to speak at an Adventist women's conference in the mountains.

The opportunity sounded awesome, so I agreed. Then, the more I began to think about it, the more I wanted to back out. I had never been to a women's conference before. My past experiences with groups of church women at events that lasted a few hours were pretty negative. Some women like to gossip about others and say negative things about them. I didn't want to be a part of it. Suddenly, the thought of spending an entire weekend trapped at this conference with a large group of women sounded terrifying. I didn't want to go. In fact, I wanted out of speaking there.

To make matters worse, I felt God telling me to open up with my whole story before I spoke – to share my testimony about how this presentation came to be instead of just jumping right in with the heart of the presentation. I had never done that before. I had never gotten personal with an audience. In fact, I had never gotten personal with more than a couple of people in my entire life at that point. Hannah knew my story, but she was only one of two who did. How could I open up with my testimony? How could I get that personal and go so deep with people that I didn't even know? How could God even ask me to do this? He knew how private I was!

I began to pray, "God, I can't do this. Don't make me go to this conference", as the date moved closer on the calendar. I even tried to get sick to get out of going. In the grocery store, I walked close to anyone who was coughing in hopes that those germs would make it my way. After all, if I lost my voice, I definitely couldn't speak at this conference! Do you know when you actually try to get sick that it never works? Two days before I was to leave for this event I was as healthy as usual.

I called my friend Hannah who had been influential in setting up my speaking engagement at this conference and began to ask her all sorts of crazy questions.

"What do people wear there?"

I was hoping that she would tell me that they dressed up the entire weekend because that would give me an excuse not to go since I didn't own any dressy clothes. I'm a jeans and t-shirt kind of girl! Nope, Hannah replied that most people dressed casual. I posed my next question.

"Will I have a room to myself, or will I have to share a room with strangers? She knew my insecurities with people I didn't know, so I thought that might get me off the hook for going.

"You are rooming with us," she replied.

I was out of excuses and out of time to think up more excuses. She then asked,

"You aren't backing out on this are you because we have had this planned for a long time. You have to be there!"

Fine, I would go, but I didn't have to be happy about it. A whole weekend with a large number of church women! That sounded scarier that confronting an angry mama bear to me!

The day finally arrived, and I made the drive to the location tucked back in a scenic area of the mountains with my radio blasting all the way. I made sure to turn it up even louder, with the windows down, as I pulled into the retreat center's parking lot. I wanted everyone standing around to know that I was not like those church women. I'm a redneck and proud of it! To my surprise, nobody even batted an eye. I got out of my SUV and walked toward the entrance where I saw Hannah and some members of her church standing. They smiled as they greeted me, and then Hannah began to show me around the place. She introduced me to a couple of the other speakers and gave me my itinerary. I was scheduled to speak the following afternoon after lunch.

Looking at the itinerary, I groaned. A vegetarian meal followed by a speaker then bedtime. "Wow, that sure sounds exciting," I thought. Here I was at this beautiful retreat center tucked in the heart of the Rocky Mountains. I wanted to explore outside and hike around. I looked at the packed schedule for the following day. After breakfast, the first speaker was scheduled followed by a short break then another speaker. This was followed by lunch then my speech which was then followed by a two hour outdoor break. I sure was looking forward to the following afternoon! But, I wasn't sure if I could make it that long as I wasn't a people person at that time!

That evening's speaker was a dynamic woman pastor named Dr. Hyveth Williams who preached on the book of Esther. In particular, she preached about Queen Vashti, who is only mentioned in the beginning of Esther and is known for refusing to come when the drunken king beckoned her. The title of this woman's speech was "Saying No to the Kings in Our Life"*. My attention was perked! I needed to learn how to say "no". After all, if I was better at saying "no", I wouldn't be stuck speaking here at this conference! I began to listen intently.

The speaker began by describing the scenario in the opening chapter of the book of Esther. King Xerxes threw a huge, extravagant party for his kingdom's officials that lasted 180 days. When that was over, he threw yet another party. This one was for all the people, from the greatest to the least, living in the fortress of Susa and lasted a week. There was abundance of wine, and by the king's edict, the people could have as much wine as they wanted with no limitations. On the seventh day, the king was drunk on the wine and improperly summoned Queen Vashti to appear so that he could show off her beauty to all of the men. The women were having a separate week long banquet. The king did not follow proper protocol when he summoned her, and she refused to come. Embarrassed by her refusal, the king worried that women everywhere might take Queen Vashti's lead and refuse to obey their husbands, so he decreed that she be forever banished from his presence. (Esther 1)

As I listened to the speaker recap this story that I knew so well, Esther being one of my favorite books in the Bible, I inwardly cheered for Queen Vashti for standing up to the king and not letting a bunch of drunken men ogle her. That took courage especially in the time she lived in when women were considered inferior and property to men. Then, the speaker took a twist with her sermon that I didn't see coming. The sermon suddenly wasn't about having the courage to say "no" to people; rather, it was about saying no to the "kings" in our lives: the kings of anxiety, the kings of fear; the kings of insecurity. It was about saying "no" to all of the kings that ruled my life! My life was ruled by anxiety; I had anxiety about speaking and attending the conference. My life was ruled by fear. I was afraid to share my testimony because I worried about what people would think of me if they knew my story. My life was ruled by insecurity. I constantly felt that I was not good enough.

My body filled with goosebumps as I listened to the message that I felt was directed right at me. I had prayed while driving to this conference that if God truly wanted me to share my testimony that He would give me a sign that I couldn't miss. Here was my sign! God wanted me to have the courage to say "no", but not to the things I thought I should say "no" too. He didn't want me to say "no" to new speaking opportunities or opportunities to connect with other Christian women. Rather, God wanted me to say "no" to the kings that were ruling my life. He wanted to give me courage instead of fear and doubt. He wanted to give me confidence in Him and the faith that I can do all things through Christ who strengthens me (Philippians 4:13). God didn't want my life to be ruled by fear, anxiety, and insecurity anymore. He wanted my life to be ruled by Him! He wanted me to trust Him!

I went back to my room that evening after the message, and while everyone else slept, I prayed. I knew God was speaking to me about the kings in my life, and I wanted to be obedient to Him. I decided that I would open up my presentation the next day with my testimony for the first time. I would like to say that I wasn't nervous, but the truth is I was still worried about what people would think of me. Yet, God gave me courage which does not necessarily mean the absence of fear. One can be courageous and still afraid at the same time. Having courage means that one decides that something is more important than the fear of what might happen. In my case, being obedient to God became more important that the fear of what others might think of me.

My time quickly approached to speak the next day. As I nervously set up my materials for my presentation, I glanced out in the audience. There, on the front row, sat Hannah and Katy – the only two women I knew in the room. Hannah knew my story, but Katy did not. Katy is a very wonderful, sweet woman. It made no sense that her presence disturbed me. Yet, I was so insecure that I fully expected her, along with everyone else, to walk out of the room in disgust as soon as I shared my story. I was still under the impression at this time that all of these church women had perfect lives, and that I was the only messed up one.

With my voice shaking, I nervously began to open up my speech with my testimony. I glanced over at Hannah and Katy, and, to my surprise, Katy was sitting there with a huge grin on her face! She wasn't smiling about what I was sharing about. She was smiling that I finally had the courage to share it! When I finally realized that Katy wasn't going to leave the room in disgust, I began to relax and shared my presentation. This was my first, but not last, experience with public vulnerability. To my surprise, when I finished speaking, several women approached me and shared how they were touched by my story and how listening to me share it gave them the courage to share secrets they had been holding for a long time.

I was approached by several more women later during this conference who thanked me for having the courage to share my story and described how they were inspired to be vulnerable and say “no” to the kings that were ruling their lives too. Satan doesn’t want us to be vulnerable. Satan wants us to be held in bondage to our past, to our secrets. He wants us to constantly worry about what people will think of us if they only knew. I am happy to report that presently in my life, I don’t care if the whole world knows my secrets! There is freedom in vulnerability! There is freedom in breaking strongholds! After this conference, I began to share my story at every speaking event with the same results. Both men and women approached me with tears in their eyes and were so inspired by my courage to share that they wanted to share their stories too! They wanted to break free from the past. They wanted to say “no” to the kings of fear and say “yes” to God.

I listened to an eighty year old woman share a secret she had never previously shared with anyone about being raped in her early twenties. She had lived most of her life believing Satan’s lies that it was her fault, that she was worthless. The tears were streaming down her face as she shared her story with me, yet, at the same time, she was smiling because for the first time in over sixty years, that event no longer had hold of her! She was no longer in bondage to it! She had just broken free! After sharing with me, she told her story to some of her friends a few days later. She called me to report that for the first time in sixty years, she was able to truly enjoy her time with her friends without worrying about what they might think of her if they knew her secret. They embraced her when she shared her story, and her story encouraged them to share their own secrets. Vulnerability spreads like wildfire!

God used Hannah to teach me vulnerability, and I learned to be vulnerable about my life with her in the first couple of years of being prayer partners. God used this conference to teach me to be vulnerable with people I didn't even know and to have the courage to share a difficult story. For a conference that I didn't even want to go to and that I tried to get out of, God taught me that sometimes He calls us to difficult moments for "such a time as this". (Esther 4:13) We need to trust, despite how difficult the circumstance may seem, that God's timing is always perfect and that sometimes He places us in uncomfortable situations to help accomplish His will.

Whatever you may be going through, whatever secrets you may be hiding, there is power in letting go and letting God. You don't have to hide behind walls you have created and live in bondage to the kings in your life. Regardless of what you have done or what has been done to you, there is freedom in vulnerability! God will set you free if you will just trust Him to guide your path. "Trust in the Lord with all your heart; do not depend on your own understanding. Seek His will in all you do, and He will show you which path to take" (Proverbs 3:5-6). "Give all your worries and cares to God, for He cares about you" (1 Peter 5:7).

Living in bondage to the "kings" in our lives hinders us from being who God wants us to be. Those "kings" can be fear, pride, insecurity, guilt, shame, codependency, anxiety, anger, and so much more. What kings are ruling your life? Follow the example of Queen Vashti and say "no" to the kings and "yes" to God.

> *"Who knows perhaps if you were made queen for just such a time as this?" (Esther 4:14)*

*("Saying No to the Kings in Our Lives" sermon is by Dr. Hyveth Williams)

Chapter 6: The Sand Trap

One of the great things about the Southwest is the remoteness of it. One can literally go days without seeing another person. I was recently in a remote area of Canyonlands National Park. When most people picture a National Park, they imagine paved roads and lots of tourists with Nikons. While that may be true in nearby Arches National Park, Canyonlands is a different story. There are two "tourist" areas in Canyonlands National Park: Island in the Sky and the Needles District. Island in the Sky is the most accessible while the Needles District has one main road and about fifty miles of four-wheel drive roads. There is also a third district named The Maze which is even more remote and only accessible by four-wheel drive vehicles. Visitors are warned at the park entrance to expect towing fees in excess of $1000 and to not expect the park rangers to help them with their vehicles.

The four-wheel drive roads are a mixture of rock, sand, and dirt which requires some driving skill and knowledge. It's very important in sandy areas to reduce tire pressure, keep your speed up, and use higher gears. Don't spin the tires, and don't brake until you are clear of the sand to help prevent you from getting stuck. On a recent trip, I drove a four-wheel drive road in Canyonlands to a remote trailhead that split off into two canyons. To get to this particular trailhead, I had to drive over a large area of sand. When I arrived, the parking lot was empty. I chose the canyon on the left to explore and enjoyed a twelve mile hike that day. The scenery was amazing, and the solitude was wonderful. It was springtime, and there was some water in the canyon bed which added to the scenery. There were also some fun pockets of quicksand which by the way can literally suck the soles off of your hiking boots! I learned that lesson in Arizona!

That evening as I returned to the trailhead where I had parked my SUV, I noticed four hikers emerge out of the other canyon on their way back to their vehicles as well. We shared hellos and chatted with each other about the canyons we had explored and then got into our three separate SUV's. Our three vehicles made a single-file line, with me in the middle, as we drove down the four-wheel drive road. Suddenly the SUV in front of me came to a stop. A young woman, tears streaming down her face, had flagged the driver down. She apparently had tried to drive her sedan through the sand, but when her tires began to spin, she got scared. Instead of backing up, she attempted to turn around in the sand and got majorly stuck. The more she pushed the accelerator, the more the tires spun. The more the tires spun; the deeper her sedan sank in the soft sand. It was buried almost to the engine! She had been sitting there waiting for help for hours not knowing when or if anyone would drive that road. There is no cell service in the backcountry to call for help.

The five of us got out of our vehicles to help and thankfully were all prepared for backcountry driving with hand spades, shovels, and tow rope. Tired as we all were from a long hike in the desert, we began to dig. We used our shovels to try to free up the front end of her vehicle enough to slip a tow rope or chain on. The problem with digging in soft sand is that the sand quickly fills back in the hole. The woman seemed to be in shock as she watched us attempt to free her vehicle. Even with the five of us digging, we were not able to make much progress after digging for an hour. Her car was buried quite deep in the soft sand!

Suddenly, we heard the sound of a vehicle approaching. Two park rangers driving a F150 truck were on their way to the trailhead to check hiking permits. They immediately noticed the problem and began to help. Finally, we were able to free the vehicle enough to attach the tow straps. The park rangers used their heavy duty truck to pull her out of the sand even though the Canyonlands policy at the Visitor Center clearly stated that their park rangers will not help with stuck vehicles. Those park rangers went above and beyond their job that day to help the stranded woman!

The really awesome part of this event is that God did not send just one person to help this woman, He sent a fleet! I totally would have tried my hardest to help her, but I would not have been able to get her vehicle out on my own. In fact, the five of us couldn't get her out. It took seven people to get her vehicle out of the sand! God orchestrated the details so that seven people would be in this remote area at the same time just to help this one woman! The park rangers said that they didn't even patrol this area daily and that this was not their normal day or time to drive this road to check permits. God sent five of us in the backcountry and timed it perfectly so that we would return from hiking in separate canyons at the same time. God orchestrated the details so that the rangers would choose that particular time and day to check permits in this remote area. This was not a coincidence of circumstances. This was an example of God's perfect timing and His working in our lives!

I don't know if this young woman was a Christian. I don't know if she truly understood what God had just done for her. She was definitely very grateful for our help and for the fact that she wouldn't have to spend the night in her stuck vehicle. If I was her, I know that I would have been very worried about the tow charge in excess of $1000 too! I'm not sure if she realized the depths of God's love for her that He would send that many strangers to help her. God had a plan for her, and it wasn't to remain stuck alone in the Utah desert!

Maybe you are feeling stuck up to your engine in sand today, and no matter how much shoveling you do to try to get out, the hole keeps filling back in. When we are stuck, it feels hopeless. Without Jesus, we are stuck in spiritual darkness. Isaiah 59:9-10 puts it this way.

"We look for light but find only darkness. We look for bright skies but walk in gloom. We grope like the blind along a wall feeling our way like people without eyes. Even at brightest noontime, we stumble as though it were dark."

Have you ever felt spiritually stuck? The first step is to repent of your sins. God promises in 1 John 1:9, "If we confess our sins, He is faithful and just and will forgive us or sins and purify us from all unrighteousness"(NIV). Don't miss the word "all"! There is nothing you have done that God in His grace and mercy won't forgive you for. You are not too messed up or too far gone! No matter what you have done, God in His grace and mercy will forgive you and cleanse you from the inside out. You don't have to remain spiritually stuck!

Are you feeling stuck in the problems of this world? God declares the following in Jeremiah 29:11-13.

"For I know the plans I have for you. They are plans for good and not for disaster, to give you a future and a hope. When you pray, I will listen. When you look for Me wholeheartedly, you will find Me."

We can trust despite our circumstances that God is still in control!

Paul understood that true joy in Christ is not based upon circumstances when he wrote the book of Philippians. Paul was in prison when he wrote a book about finding joy in Jesus. He knew that God was using his circumstances, and how he was responding to them, in a mighty way to draw others to Him. Paul was speaking from the heart when he wrote:

"Don't worry about anything; instead, pray about everything. Tell God what you need, and thank Him for all He has done. Then you will experience God's peace, which exceeds anything we can understand. His peace will guard your hearts and minds as you live in Christ Jesus." (Philippians 4:6-7)

When you are overcome by anxiety, don't let those anxious thoughts consume you. Instead, begin praying, praising, and thanking God for His goodness. It is hard to focus on the negative when you turn your thoughts to God. We are all going to have times when we feel overwhelmed and stuck. The important thing to remember is that God is still in control and that He orchestrates details to achieve His purposes. Who knows, maybe He will send a fleet to rescue you too!

"For I know the plans I have for you. They are plans for good and not for disaster, to give you a future and a hope. When you pray, I will listen. When you look for Me wholeheartedly, you will find Me." (Jeremiah 29:11-13)

Chapter 7: Peace in the Storm

I went to a remote section of the Sangre de Christos mountain range for an epic birthday adventure last year with a plan to solo hike to several mining ruins and ghost towns at high elevation. I checked the weather models before I left on the trip. There was no warning of what was to come. Saturday was beautiful in the low 60's. I woke up Sunday, on my birthday, in my tent perched on some mining tailings at 9870 feet, to partly cloudy skies and chilly conditions. I was wearing hiking pants and a long-sleeve shirt with a thin jacket as I set off to ascend seven miles to some ruins perched on the mountainside at 11,870 feet. Midway through the day, the weather changed drastically. The sun disappeared as the temperature rapidly dropped, and the wind began gusting. I wasn't concerned as cold, windy temperatures are often the case at higher elevations. However, the overcast skies soon began sleeting, then snowing. The wind began to blow with hurricane force winds. I was soon caught in a white-out!

I had left my balaclava, snow pants, and goggles behind in my tent not having foreseen that I would need them that day as the temperature was supposed to have been in the 50's with no storm predicted. Caught in a sudden white-out on the mountainside at nearly 12,000 feet, I soon regretted that decision! Thankfully, there was no prior snow on the ground where I was, and temperatures had been warm enough previously that it wasn't sticking yet. Even though I couldn't see much in front of me in the whiteout, I was able to slowly descend by staring at the ground under my feet. The smooth dirt of the old mining road was still evident. I was glad to look down as the biting wind and snow pelting my face hurt when I tried to look forward.

The strong, bitter wind pelted the snow against my face like tiny pieces of gravel, and my exposed extremities soon began to turn bright red and burn -a sign of frostbite. After a few hours of descending, I finally made it back to my camp at 9870 feet and crawled into my sleeping bag to warm up. By this point, my legs were bright red and literally burning under the thin hiking pants I wore, as were my fingers and my face. My skin literally felt on fire! I quickly changed clothes and covered myself from head to toe while ripping open several packets of emergency instant heat and placing them on various parts of my body. I filled up my pee bottle with hot urine and stuffed that in the sleeping bag with me as well to help generate warmth. The wind was still raging outside my tent, and the whiteout showed no sign of abating. I had my satellite communicator with me, but I knew that even if I pushed the emergency button which would transmit my precise location to a global network of Search and Rescue responders that they would have to wait until the storm diminished before they would be able to go into such a remote area to rescue me.

I was all alone, caught in an unexpected whiteout

on a remote mountainside in the Sangre de Christos forty-five miles from the nearest "town" (30 miles on dirt roads and 15 miles on high clearance roads) with nobody else around. I tried talking aloud, and my speech was slightly slurred - a beginning sign of hypothermia. My skin was still bright red and burning horribly, and I was shivering uncontrollably. Despite the warmth of the layers, the sleeping bag, and my pee bottle, I just could not get warm. I began to panic knowing that I was in a very bad situation and wished that I had a companion with me.

Then I realized that I wasn't really alone. God was with me! The same God who created the wind, the snow, the freezing cold, and the whiteout conditions! Recalling a sermon I recently heard about thanking God even in hard times, I began to thank Him for His power, His majesty, and His might. I began to praise Him for letting me witness and experience firsthand the force of His power. As I began to do that, the panicked feelings went away, and I was filled with peace that made no sense at all.

I had absolute peace despite the fact that I was facing frostbite! I had absolute peace despite the fact that I was shivering from the cold! I had absolute peace despite the wind raging outside my tent and despite knowing that help was miles and miles away! As absurd as it sounds, I had peace in the midst of a storm!

Slowly beginning to warm up some in the cocoon I had made of my sleeping bag with the help of the emergency heat packets and my pee bottle, I began to read through the Psalms, reading aloud so that I could keep tabs on my speech. I wanted to know if it was still slurred. I soon began to joyfully sing songs of praise.

What had been a horrible way to spend my birthday soon became an awesome, epic adventure! I was truly having a good time waiting out the whiteout in my tent on the mountainside. How many people get to experience the force of nature like this firsthand? It was seriously cool - and a God thing that it was no longer scary!

This storm wasn't even in the forecast when I had set off on this trip. I had no idea how long the storm would continue, but I was relatively warm covered head to toe in my winter clothes while cocooned in my sleeping bag in my tent. I was still cold but not freezing. The storm raged on throughout the afternoon, evening, and night, but I was truly making the best of it while reading my Bible and a novel in my tent. After a restless night of dozing off and on, I awoke to blessed sunshine! Warmth finally! I have never been happier to feel the rays of the sun on me as I was that morning!

I had a couple of patches of mild frostbite, but otherwise I came through unscathed! I truly had the experience of a lifetime on my birthday, one I never will forget. It was absolutely awesome to see and photograph the snow on the mountainside the next couple of days and know that it came from a blizzard that I had barely survived. I got to spend my birthday with God and see His power in action while experiencing His unexplainable peace in the midst of a terrifying storm! Truly amazing!

The Bible promises us that we can experience true peace despite our circumstances, and I experienced that firsthand. I was facing frostbite, hypothermia, and even dehydration as my water froze with the drastic change in temperature. Yet, despite all of those factors,

I had peace –true, unexplainable peace! I had peace in knowing that God was with me and that I wasn't alone. I had peace in knowing that no matter what happened, God would help me deal with it. Because of that, I was able to be perfectly happy reading a book and singing songs in my tent in the middle of a whiteout even though I had no idea how long it would last.

Jesus's disciples experienced a fierce, dangerous storm while Jesus was right there with them. They were panicking at their circumstances while Jesus was sleeping. In anger, they shouted, "Don't you care that we are going to drown?" Jesus's response to them was simply, "Why are you afraid? Do you still have no faith?" (Mark 4:35-41)

His disciples had seen him perform many miracles. They had seen Him do the impossible by casting out demons and healing people with leprosy, yet they were afraid in the storm with Jesus right there with them. It is easy to display faith when times are good. The test happens when the storms come and the doubts and fears we keep hidden inside are revealed. We ask ourselves over and over, "Does God really care what I am going through?"

You might be caught in an emotional blizzard and facing situations that are just as drastic and serious to you as frostbite and hypothermia were to me. Have you ever felt caught by surprise by an uncontrollable storm? Have you ever been pelted with grief, hurt, pain, loneliness, sadness, and shame? God knew that we would get overwhelmed by storms and lose sight of the warmth of the coming of a new morning. By focusing our thoughts on God's promises to us, we can have peace while the storm rages on.

"God is our refuge and strength, always ready to help in times of trouble. So we will not fear when earthquakes come and the mountains crumble into the sea." (Psalm 46:1-2)

(snowshoeing near a frozen waterfall)

Chapter 8: Blurred Vision

I enjoy introducing people to caving, especially children. I have nothing against tourist caves with their electric lighting and concrete steps, but there is something about true caving that makes one walk away in wonder. Seeing a cave in its natural setting with only the light of a headlamp shining from your helmet as you are covered from head to toe in mud is adventure at its finest. In fact, cavers will tell you that caving is truly the final frontier here on earth! There are still unknown caves and passageways yet to be discovered. A caver, even in this day of age, still has the potential of being the first to step foot in a cavern. Caving is an explorer's dream!

Don't make the mistake of calling a caver a spelunker however. A spelunker is a beginner caver who doesn't really know what he is doing. A caver is a serious explorer who shows respect for the cave environment and formations as he hopes and dreams of finding a part of a cave that nobody has ever discovered. Caves are wonderful and filled with mystical formations that God has created, yet caves are also very fragile and in need of protection. Touching a cave formation with one's bare hands can cause that formation that has been forming for hundreds of years to die simply because of the body oils that are on all of our skin. Caving requires preparation not only for our own safety but for the cave's safety as well. We are responsible for protecting it for future generations to enjoy. Sadly, people have not always had that mindset, and there are many caves that have been ruined over the years by senseless graffiti and breakage of fragile formations.

In addition to speaking engagements, I lead caving expeditions on a voluntary basis. I introduce people to the physical aspects of caving as I incorporate spiritual analogies that can be drawn from being in a cave of darkness in an effort to show them their need for Jesus. True caving involves risk of injury to oneself or to other cavers. I explain this in advance as I have the adults sign waivers releasing me from all liability. I also spend the first part of the caving "tour" going over safety procedures to follow in the cave such as using three points of contact at all times, no jumping, and keeping a short distance from the person in front of you so you don't accidentally get kicked.

Despite all of my talks on safety, sometimes, especially with children, something can go wrong as it did on a caving trip I led two years ago. I had just bouldered my way down a three-tiered pitch in the cave and gotten into position to spot my group. A nine year old girl standing about fifteen feet above me at the top of the pitch was holding a backpack. She was supposed to toss the pack down to me when I told her. However, being a hyperactive nine year old, she let the pack fall just as I was looking up at the group. As the pack covered in mud fell, a huge glob of mud mixed with tiny pebbles hit me in both eyes. I suddenly could not see at all! Plus, it hurt very badly!

I crouched down on the slippery cave surface totally scared because I suddenly could not see a thing and worried because there were four people (one adult, two teenagers, and the 9 year old) standing above me on that ledge depending on me to help them down that pitch and out of the cave. My clothing was covered in mud as usual; caving is a very muddy activity. I frantically began to pull out my thermal layer, which was the only article of clothing I had on that wasn't covered in mud, and started wiping and dabbing my eyes with it. I couldn't see at all! I was terrified! The pain in my eyes was intense. I prayed over and over, "God, help me! Help me please!"

I could hear the group above me talking amongst themselves having no idea their guide below them was in such a predicament. This was their first time in a cave; they wouldn't be able to find their way out on their own much less get help. I blinked and dabbed my eyes with my thermal shirt for about ten minutes while experiencing intense eye pain. I was quietly panicking and worrying about becoming blind because of this. Finally, my vision began to slowly return. I could make out a little light from my headlamp although my vision was very blurry. It was too blurry to cave for sure. I continued to pray as I dabbed my eyes on my thermal shirt. They began watering terribly at this point. At last, I could see again although my eyes were still watering intensely. I looked down at my thermal shirt with the beam of my headlamp and was amazed at the amount of dirt on it that had been wiped from my eyes.

God is so good! I had contacts on and even they weren't damaged by the mud and tiny pebbles! The fact that there was no damage to my eyes at all was nothing short of a miracle! I was finally able to stand back up, calmly spot everyone down that pitch, and lead them out of the cave. My eyes were red rimmed and swollen looking, but my vision seemed to be fine. I arranged a visit with my eye doctor when I returned home who examined my eyes and pronounced them fine with no damage.

My experience with temporary blindness caused me to think of the story in Mark about Jesus healing a blind man:

"When they arrived at Bethsaida, some people brought a blind man to Jesus, and they begged him to touch the man and heal him. Jesus took the blind man by the hand and led him out of the village. Then, spitting on the man's eyes, He laid His hands on him and asked, 'Can you see anything now?'

The man looked around, 'Yes,' he said, 'I see people, but I can't see them very clearly. They look like trees walking around.'

Then Jesus placed His hands on the man's eyes again, and his eyes were opened. His sight was completely restored, and he could see everything clearly." (Mark 8:22-25)

This is the only time that Jesus healed someone in stages. It's like a two-part miracle. The question is, "Why did He heal the man in stages?" Was it because Jesus failed to heal him correctly the first time? Well, if you have read the Scriptures, you know that can't be true. Jesus never failed at anything! Jesus had a purpose for everything that He did, and I believe that

He had a lesson that He was trying to convey here.

If you take this passage in context, at the beginning of Mark 8 (vs. 1-8), Jesus had just done an amazing miracle in the wilderness with seven loaves of bread and three small fish. He not only multiplied it to feed a crowd of four thousand people, but He even made sure that there were seven large baskets of leftover food! He had just shown His power to provide in a mighty way! Yet, by verse 14, the disciples were hungry again and were arguing because they only had one loaf of bread in their boat even though Jesus was right there with them. They had just watched him recently make a huge miracle out of seven loaves of bread and were suddenly worried over one loaf! Had I been one of them, I would have been all like, "Okay Jesus do your thing!" Instead, they worried.

Jesus fussed at them in verses 16-21:

"At this they began to argue with each other because they hadn't brought any bread. Jesus knew what they were saying, so He said, 'Why are you arguing about having no bread? Don't you know or understand even yet? Are your hearts too hard to take it in? You have eyes – can't you see? You have ears – can't you hear? Don't you remember anything at all? When I fed the 5,000 with five loaves of bread, how many baskets of leftovers did you pick up afterwards?'

'Twelve,' they said.

'And when I fed the 4,000 with seven loaves, how many large baskets of leftovers did you pick up?'

'Seven,' they said.

'Don't you understand yet?' he asked them." (Mark 8:16-21)

They saw it, but they just didn't get it. They had eyes that were fully functional, but still they couldn't see that Jesus would provide no matter how drastic their circumstances appeared. Jesus's healing of the blind man occurred after this.

It is possible to have eyes and not see clearly. I know because I am nearsighted. Without contacts or eyeglasses, anything that is not directly two inches in front of my face is distorted and blurred. I can look at my computer screen without contacts or glasses, but I cannot see the words on it. I can look at people, but they look like blurred images walking around. I have eyes, but without vision correction, I cannot see. That is what this blind man experienced when Jesus partially healed him in stage one. He could see, but he could not see clearly. Is halfway good enough? How comfortable would you feel if I attempted to drive a vehicle without vision correction? Or lead you out of a cave with blurred vision?

The same is true spiritually. Sometimes we need spiritual vision correction! We see God, but we don't see Him clearly because we put Him in a box and expect Him to perform and conform to our image of Him. When He doesn't, we get angry at Him. He let us down, we think. Did He really let us down, or did we just not see or understand His purpose in the first place? Spiritual growth does not happen instantly. We are used to getting things instantly because of the world we live in. But, God doesn't work that way. Spiritual growth takes time, and it takes stages. It is easy to compare ourselves with other Christians and think, "Why don't I have their level of faith? Why haven't I made as much spiritual progress as her?" All along our spiritual journeys, Jesus is asking us, "Do you see Me yet? Do you truly see Me yet? Not as what you have been taught about Me. Not as what you have imagined Me to be. But, do you truly see Me as I am?"

God also wants us to be honest with Him. This man could have settled for partial vision and told Jesus that it was fine. Instead, He told the truth, "I see people, but I can't see them very clearly. They look like trees walking around." (Mark 8: 24) Are you being honest with God? Have you told Him, as the father of the possessed boy did in Mark 9:24, "I do believe, but help me overcome my unbelief!" Have you cried out as the psalmist did in Psalm 119:18, "Open my eyes to see!"? Are you truly seeing God and His truths? Are you seeing God with 20/20 spiritual vision, or are you seeing Him partially through blurred vision. Cry out to Him today to open up the eyes of your heart so that you can truly see Him!

"I see people, but I can't see them very clearly. They look like trees walking around." (Mark 8: 24

(stalactites in a cave)

Part 3: The Analogies

Chapter 1: Let God Be Your Belayer

God has not blessed me with children of my own, but I am blessed to be a nanny to some very sweet boys. I am frequently asked how I find the time to do all that I do: hiking, photography, speaking, writing, etc. There is no secret formula. Truthfully, it is just all a balancing act. God has really blessed me with this nanny position, and I only take care of the boys on a part-time basis. I get to be the fun one who comes over, plays with them all day, and takes them to fun activities. I really have it made! How many people can truthfully say that they love going to work? I honestly can say that!

One activity that I have introduced the boys to is climbing on an indoor rock wall. I took the two older boys when they were three and nine years old to an indoor recreation center where there is a twenty-five foot climbing wall. I am belay-certified, but the youngest age that I previously had belayed was ten years old simply because most places do not have full body harnesses that will fit small children. I was excited to find out this particular place did. Matt was three years old at the time, and this was his first experience at being “roped in”. Both Matt and Justin were excited about getting on the climbing wall, but how they each faced the challenge was very interesting.

Matt was not afraid at all! I showed him how to lean back in his harness on the rope, and he eagerly began climbing up the wall while enjoying "flying" (as he put it) back to the ground on the rope. He had no fear whatsoever! On the other hand, Justin, the nine year old, wanted to climb but was afraid at the same time of letting go of the rocks on the wall. He climbed up a few feet and froze over and over. Refusing to lean back in his harness and kick off the wall to descend, he chose instead to lower himself by hands and feet each time while shaking tremendously in fear. As a result, while Matt was having an awesome time climbing up the wall as far as he could go and "flying" down it over and over, Justin was unable to climb more than five feet above the ground because he was paralyzed by a fear of falling. It took many tries to convince him that he was perfectly safe and would not fall. Over and over, I encouraged him to let go of the wall, lean back in his harness, and trust me as his belayer. Finally, he made a leap of faith and let go of the wall instead of clinging to it for dear life. When he realized that he wasn't going to fall but would remain basically suspended there in the air, the countenance on his face visually changed from fear to confidence. Finally, he was able to climb all the way to the top and ring the bell!

As I took turns belaying them and thinking about the differences in how they were approaching climbing, God gave me a spiritual lesson. Why was Matt, the three year old, not afraid to let go of the wall like his older brother? The answer was simple. Matt trusted me implicitly! I have taken care of him since he was a few weeks old. He trusts me, loves me, and knows that I am there for him. We have a relationship, a bond, with each other in that sense. Whereas, even though I have known his older brother, Justin, just as long as I have known Matt, I haven't spent much time with him. Justin and I don't have the same kind of relationship built on trust that Matt and I have. Matt's absolute trust in me to take care of him and keep him safe is an analogy of what it means to have a childlike faith in God.

The Bible talks about the importance of having the faith of a child in Matthew 18:2-4.

"Jesus called a little child to Him and put the child among them. Then He said, I tell you the truth, unless you turn from your sins and become like little children, you will never get into the Kingdom of Heaven. So anyone who becomes as humble as this little child is the greatest in the Kingdom of Heaven."

A childlike faith in God means trusting that God is going to be there for you even in circumstances that you have never experienced before. The climbing wall was new to Matt, yet he completely trusted me to not let him fall because he knew, based on past experiences, that I was going to take care of him.

It required a lot of trust on Justin's part to let go of the wall and trust me as his belayer to not let him fall. It is really hard to trust someone that you don't know very well and don't have a strong relationship with. As a certified belayer, I basically, in a sense, have someone's life in my hands. If I was not paying attention, the person that I am belaying could fall and become seriously injured if I let go of the rope or did not brake the rope in the manner that I should. It does take a serious amount of trust to let go of the wall and trust your belayer to get you safely down. I struggle with that myself when I allow others to belay me that haven't belayed me before. It is hard because the constant questions running through my mind are, "Is he paying attention? Does she know what she is doing? Can I truly trust this person with my life?" It is difficult to trust that your belayer has everything under control if you don't have a relationship built on past experiences and trust with that person!

Sadly, most of us do not have a childlike faith in God because we are afraid to trust Him. We are more like the nine year old: independent, afraid to trust, and afraid to let go. As a result, we take one step forward and two steps back as we are caught in a constant struggle for peace that only God can give. We move from relationship to relationship, job after job, goal after goal – constantly seeking more but never truly happy, never truly satisfied, and never truly at peace. The reason is that we don't really trust God. We haven't let go of the climbing wall. We are clinging to our own abilities instead of God's abilities.

Maybe you are afraid to trust God because you have been let down by an earthly father and are afraid to trust a Heavenly Father. You may have experienced unspeakable trials in your life and wondered why a loving God did not intervene. I will be the first to admit that I do not have all the answers. However, I can tell you that the truth about God's love is His promise to be right beside us through it all in every circumstance good or bad. God has promised in Deuteronomy 31:8 that He will never leave us or forsake us.

"The Lord Himself goes before you and will be with

you; He will never leave you nor forsake you. Do not be afraid; do not be discouraged." (Deut. 31:6 NIV)

Jesus says in John 16:33 that there will be troubles, trials, and hard times in this world, yet we can take heart and be courageous because He has overcome. We can have the same childlike faith in God that Matt does in me. We can believe God's promise that He will always be with us wherever we are. As vigilant as I am with Matt, as carefully as I watch over him, accidents happen. There have been times when he has gotten scrapes, cuts, and bruises. When that happens, he runs to me because he knows that I will kiss his 'owies', bandage his wounds, and comfort him. In the same manner, God is beside us when we are hurt, sad, or lonely. He is there waiting for us to run to Him for comfort.

Even though Matt has had 'owies' happen in the past, he still trusts me as his friend. He still runs to me for comfort when he is sad or hurt because he knows, as his friend, that I love him. He doesn't shout, "You were right there with me, and I got hurt anyway! You must not care about me! I am never going to trust you again!" as we do to God sometimes. Matt understands that accidents happen. He understands that even though I am walking right beside him, he can still trip and fall. He understands that as his friend, I am going to be there for him and help him through whatever he may be going through because I love him.

That is what having a childlike faith in God means. It means trusting God and understanding that even though circumstances don't always work out the way that we want them to and even though bad things sometimes happen because we live in a fallen world,

God still cares, loves us, and hurts for us. How many times have you angrily turned from God because you felt that if He truly cared, you never should have gotten hurt or had to experience a trial? How many times have you missed the fact that He was right there next to you all along waiting for you to turn to Him for comfort?

We are all, in essence, on a climbing wall in life. We can tightly grip the rocks, trying to be in control while doing things all on our own, and never find true joy and peace. Or, we can take a leap of faith, let go of that wall, and trust God. We can trust God with our worries! We can trust God with our problems, our struggles, our fears, our relationships, and our insecurities! When we finally take that leap of faith, choose to trust God, give Him our doubts and fears, and let Him be in control of our lives instead of us, we experience what Justin eventually experienced on the climbing wall: pure joy.

"I pray that God the source of hope will fill you completely with joy and peace because you trust in Him. Then you will overflow with confident hope through the power of the Holy Spirit." (Romans 15:13)

Will you let God be your belayer today? Will you let go of that unsatisfying grip you have on the wall of life and trust God to hold you? Will you believe that the same power that resurrected Jesus from the dead can resurrect and transform your heart and life (Romans 8:11)? Will you believe that He will change you in ways that you never could have imagined (Ephesians 4:20)? Will you pray God's promises over your life and truly believe them? "Give your cares, worries, and anxieties to God because He cares for you." (1 Peter 5:7) God loves you. He cares for you. You can trust Him! Let God be your belayer!

"Give your cares, worries, and anxieties to God because He cares for you." (1 Peter 5:7)

Chapter 2: Things Aren't Always What They Seem

I do not like shopping, especially clothes shopping. Yet, I have to buy jeans every once in a while because they wear out. One day I walked into a popular clothing store and stared in dismay at nine different styles of jeans. I most certainly did not want to take the time to try on all of them just to see which one fit me the best. A very helpful sales lady walked up and asked if she could assist me. I explained to her that I just wanted a comfortable pair of boot cut jeans. She handed me one that was size 4 and walked with me toward the dressing room. I tried to hand her the jeans back while laughing.

"Umm, there's no way I can fit into those. I need at least a size 8."

She replied, "I am pretty sure that a 4 will work for you with room to spare."

Me: "There is no way I can fit into that! I need at least an 8 but probably a 10."

Frowning a bit, she insisted, "This will fit you fine. I am sure of it!"

I didn't think so. I don't have a very good body image and avoid full body mirrors for that reason. I feel like I am the width of an Oompa Loompa from the original “Charlie and the Chocolate Factory”. This lady must not have had eyes as she continued to insist that the jeans she handed me would fit me “with room to spare”. Doubtful, I walked into the dressing room sure that I would not be able to pull the jeans up past my hips. I stared at the full-body mirror in disgust at my huge calves and elephant hips. How could this woman possibly think that I could fit into size 4 jeans? I mean, seriously, didn’t she take a good look at me? Didn’t she see how huge I am? Did she not see my huge butt?

To my surprise, the jeans fit just as she told me they would, “with room to spare”! The mirror had lied to me, and my mind had lied to me. In my mind’s image, I am much larger than I actually am. Sometimes the mirror lies to us! Sometimes what we think we see in the mirror is not factual; it is not what others see when they look at us. When I look in a mirror, I don’t see the actual size I am, I see an Oompa Loompa. I don’t see the truth regarding my weight, but the saleslady did. Not only did she see the truth, she also would not let me live a lie. She could have handed me the size 8 that I asked for and let me buy jeans that were too baggy on me like I usually do to hide my imaginary weight. Instead, she kindly pointed out the truth to me. I didn’t need a size 8; I needed a size 4.

What do you see when you look in the mirror? Maybe you don’t have trouble with self-image and see an Oompa Loompa looking back at you like I do. Instead, you see shame, guilt, failures, hurt, loneliness, and worthlessness. You wonder if anyone could possibly truly want you, or if God could actually use you. Satan is that mirror, and he is constantly whispering lies to us! He wants us to think that we are too messed up, too broken, and too used up to be any good to others or to God. Just like the mirror constantly gives me false images of myself, Satan gives us false images too that we mistake for truth. The negative words pound at us.

"No one could ever want you after what you have done. You are a failure! You are not good enough to be a Christian. You are too messed up for God! It is your entire fault. You have ruined every relationship you have touched. You want to lead a Bible Study with your past? What a joke!"

Sound familiar? Satan lies to us, just like the mirror lies. When I look in the mirror, I see a distorted reflection of myself, and that is what Satan tries to give us with his lies. He distorts the facts. The truth is that things aren't always what they seem. Satan wants you to think that God is condemning you for your past, your mistakes, and your failures. The truth is that God does not repetitively condemn us! Sure, He points out our mistakes, but then He just says, "Repent! Don't do it again." Picture the story from John 8 about the woman caught in adultery.

"Teacher," they said to Jesus. "This woman was caught in the act of adultery. The law of Moses says to stone her. What do you say?'

There were trying to trap Him into saying something they could use against Him, but Jesus stooped down and wrote in the dust with His finger. They kept demanding an answer, so He stood up again and said, "All right, but let the one who has never sinned throw the first stone!" Then He stooped down again and wrote in the dust.

When the accusers heard this, they slipped away one by one, beginning with the oldest, until only Jesus was left in the middle of the crowd with the woman. Then Jesus stood up again and said to the woman, "Where are your accusers? Didn't even one of them condemn you?"

"No, Lord," she said.

And Jesus said, "Neither do I. Go and sin no more."

(John 8: 4-11)

Wait a minute! Doesn't God condemn us? Isn't He ready to strike us down for even the tiniest mistake? That is what Satan would have us to believe. But, if that is true, why did Jesus spare this woman? Why didn't He stone her?

First of all, this woman's accusers were only presenting a half-truth to Jesus. Technically, the law of Moses stated to stone both the man and woman caught in adultery (Leviticus 20:10). They seemed so concerned for the Law to be upheld, yet the man that the woman had been with was suspiciously not present. These accusers were simply using this woman as a convenient pawn in an attempt to trap Jesus.

Who was this woman? The Bible doesn't state her name. I propose that she is you, and she is me. I am not saying that we have all committed adultery like this woman. Yet, at some point in our lives, we have all been "caught" in our sins just like her. It is easy to point our self-righteous fingers at others, but it doesn't feel so good when we get caught sinning, does it? It is shameful and embarrassing!

This woman was spared because God is full of grace, mercy, and forgiveness. I believe that Jesus taught this woman's accusers a lesson here. Have you ever thought about what He was writing in the dust? Could it possibly have been the sins of those present? Could it possibly have been that once they saw their sins written there for all to see, they left in shame and embarrassment?

"For everyone has sinned; we all fall short of God's glorious standard" (Romans 3:23).

Jesus offered hope to the woman remaining. He did not condemn her although He certainly had the right, since He was the only one there who had never sinned. Instead, He told her, "I don't condemn you either. Repent, and don't do this again."

The Bible states if we confess our sins (1 John 1:9), repent (which means to turn from our sin and go a whole different direction), and ask forgiveness, God will cleanse us from the inside out and remove our sins as far as the east is from the west (Psalm 103:12). In fact, He promises, that He won't even remember our sins any more (Hebrews 10:17)! He doesn't bring it back up to us after we have repented and been forgiven. If you are being constantly reminded of sins that you have already repented of and asked forgiveness for, that is Satan condemning you and not God! Oh, he would like you to think that it is God condemning you, but just like the mirror, things are not always what they seem!

When we turn to God and ask Him to take control of our hearts and lives, God creates a whole new person in us!

"Anyone who belongs to Christ has become a new person. The old life is gone; a new life has begun!" (2 Corinthians 5:17)

What lies do you believe about yourself? What do you see when you look in the mirror? Do you see a messed-up, broken, worthless individual? Or, do you see a child of the living God who has been set free? "If the Son sets you free, you are truly free" (John 8:36). Don't live in bondage to Satan's lies. Also, don't enable others to stay in that bondage. Do your best to convince others of the truth of God's love just like the sales lady convinced me that I really did not need size 8 jeans!

"Neither do I condemn you. Go and sin no more." (John 8:11)

Chapter 3: Dance in the Rain

Being a nanny is sometimes very stressful as anyone who provides care for young children knows. Some days, things just do not go right. When Matt was two years old, he was in the process of being 'potty'-trained. One day I was cuddling Sam, the baby, and feeding him a bottle when Matt suddenly said, "Poop!" Not wanting to miss this opportunity to get him to go in the toilet instead of his diapers, I quickly put Sam in his cradle, picked Matt up, and rushed him to the bathroom. He had one of those seats that inserts on top of the toilet seat to make him feel like a big boy. I handed him his 'potty' book to read and hurried back to the living room where I could hear Sam loudly complaining over his meal being interrupted. I picked him up and began to feed him once more. Just then, I heard Matt cry out from the bathroom, "I'm done!" He didn't know how to get off the toilet by himself, so he was basically stuck there on top of the toilet.

I reassured Matt, "Just a minute. Your brother is almost finished with his bottle." I did not want to interrupt Sam's bottle again. Two year olds have no patience, however. Matt hollered once more,

"I'M DONE!"

"Just a minute," I called back. Matt stopped yelling for me to come get him, so I assumed that he was reading his 'potty' book quietly. Wait a minute. What was I thinking? Matt is never quiet! I quickly laid Sam in his cradle and hurried to the bathroom. My jaw dropped as I surveyed the huge mess Matt had made all while sitting on the toilet. Apparently, he got bored reading his 'potty' book and somehow managed to unroll the entire roll of toilet paper into a huge pile under his feet. He smiled mischievously at me and pointed to his two dinosaurs that he had thrown on top of the mess and said, "Dinosaur trouble!" insinuating that the dinosaurs had made the huge mess and were in big trouble.

Sam was unhappy at being left alone in his cradle and screaming at the top of his lungs, so I quickly cleaned up the toilet paper mess and helped Matt off the toilet – not realizing that he actually had pooped that time and that there was some smeared on his rear. I walked with him back into the living room to grab a diaper and some wipes. He quickly climbed on the couch to get away from me because he liked to make a game out of getting his diaper put on, and that is when I noticed the poop.

I breathed the words, "Oh No!", as I headed to the couch to grab him. He thought it was a fun game and laughingly scrambled onto the floor as he tried to scoot away from me, smearing poop on the floor rug in the process. Meanwhile, Sam was still screaming at the top of his lungs to be let out of his cradle. I finally cornered Matt, cleaned him up, and placed a new diaper on him. Then, I began to scrub the poop off the carpet and couch. While I was frantically scrubbing away at the stains, Matt took advantage of the moment. He began placing stickers on the windows. I looked up at the sound of his laughter and hurriedly began removing the stickers before they became permanently stuck then resumed the task of scrubbing the stains off the couch and carpet. Meanwhile, Matt found a marker, thankfully washable, and began coloring on the wall.

Life with toddlers is unpredictable to say the least. This was one of those mornings where I could either laugh at the absurdity of the situation or cry. Tears filled my eyes. The children were out of control, and I felt like a failure as a nanny. Then, I thought of the story of Paul and Silas in the book of Acts and decided that the boys were not going to steal my joy for the day. My joy is not found in circumstances; it is found in God! I also knew that I am not a failure in God's eyes and that He will give me the strength to get through the day. So, instead of crying, I chose to laugh. The situation was quite funny after all. Sometimes Matt can definitely be a little Dennis the Menace!

I turned the radio on, picked up screaming Sam, cradled him in one arm, and put Matt on my other hip as I spontaneously began to dance and sing with them. Soon, everyone was laughing, Sam included. By the time I set the boys down, Matt seemed to have lost his mischievous attitude and began to play with his toys. What I had just experienced was peace in the midst of a storm. A morning that was obviously not going well turned into a wonderful day simply because I changed my attitude. I was frustrated with Matt's behavior. The more frustrated I got the more of a Dennis the Menace he became and the louder Sam yelled at not being the center of attention. We could have been stuck in that rut of frustration all day. However, since I chose that Matt was not going to steal my joy, spontaneously dancing and singing changed all of our attitudes for the rest of the day.

Have you experienced days where nothing seems to go right? Weeks? Months of one thing after another going wrong? Life can be stressful! We tend to want to skip those stressful times of life and spend our time happily dancing. My friend, Diane, once gave me a wonderful analogy when I was complaining to her about feeling stressed out. At that time, my landlord had let the duplex I had lived in for nine years go into foreclosure. The house was getting auctioned off, and the tenant on the other side and I had to move. It wasn't our fault. We always paid our rent on time.

"Why should my life get disrupted over someone else's mistakes?" I vented to Diane over and over on the phone. The rental market had risen over the past nine years. I was having trouble finding a nice duplex for the same amount of rent per month.

"It's not fair!" I vented to her.

Diane got quiet for a moment then responded, "We can't get stressed over the day-to-day stuff. We just do because we want to know everything. We don't like having life unfold to us. We want to skip to the back and read the last page. But, there is some good stuff in the middle."

I was stressed because the situation seemed unfair to me, and at the time, I didn't know how it would play out. I didn't know how I could afford to pay higher rent for equivalent space elsewhere. Yet, she was right. Good things can come out of hard times. It wasn't easy. I didn't enjoy having to move from my home because of my landlord's mistakes. It certainly wasn't fair! Yet, God in His infinite wisdom knew it was time for me to leave. My landlord had not kept up on the maintenance of the duplex. There were loose boards, mold issues, and the furnace was broken half the time. In fact, I was sick a lot because of the mold issues and the dampness of the house! Yet, I was willing to overlook the risks to my health because it was my home. I had been there a long time and was comfortable there.

Sometimes God moves us from situations where we have gotten too comfortable to notice that they are unhealthy for us. It may be a relationship. It may be a job or any number of situations. You may be stressed from a situation right now that you never imagined you would have to deal with. You may be raising a disabled child, taking care of an aging parent, or fighting a disease! You might have already raised your own children and suddenly find yourself raising your grandchildren just when you thought life was finally going to be about what you want for a change. It is important to remember whatever stress you may be dealing with that it is just a chapter in your life. God really does have your best interests in mind! This may seem like a very, long chapter, but there is more to your story! Don't put a period where God has only put a comma!

Sometimes, as absurd as it sounds, you just have to sing in the rain. Dance in the storm that you are in. Paul knew about dancing in a storm after he was falsely accused, beaten, and thrown into prison. How would you respond? Most people, myself included, would probably sit there feeling sorry for themselves while bemoaning the fact that it was "unfair". Not Paul and Silas! Consider this excerpt from Acts 16.

"A mob quickly formed against Paul and Silas, and the city officials ordered them stripped and beaten with wooden rods. They were severely beaten, and then they were thrown into prison. The jailer was ordered to make sure they didn't escape. So the jailer put them into the inner dungeon and clamped their feet in the stocks.

Around midnight Paul and Silas were praying and singing hymns to God, and the other prisoners were listening." (Acts 16:22-25)

Paul and Silas were in a stressful situation after having been falsely accused, beaten, and imprisoned, yet their reaction was to pray and sing songs to God. Their circumstances had gone from bad to worse, yet their attitudes remained positive and even joyful. They both realized that their joy was not based on their circumstances and instead was based on Jesus Christ. Because of that, they were able to sing in the rain. They trusted God's promises.

"God causes everything to work together for the good of those who love God and are called according to His purpose for them." (Romans 8:28)

When you are facing a stressful situation, do you tell God how big and impossible your situation is? Or, do you tell your situation how big God is? Is your joy based on circumstances? Or, is your joy based on God?

Vivian Greene, a novelist, once said, "Life is not about waiting for the storms to pass. It's about learning how to dance in the rain." Don't focus so much on the chapters ahead of or behind you that you miss out on what God is trying to teach you, or do through you, in the chapter that you are in. Learn how to dance in the rain. Sing and praise God through hard times! Paul and Silas were a witness to everyone in that jail cell. The jailer and his family became a part of the family of God because of the joyous faith that Paul and Silas exhibited. There is good stuff in the middle!

"When troubles come your way, consider it an opportunity for great joy" (James 1:2).

Chapter 4: Memorials in our lives

I enjoy riding my mountain bike on the many trails here in Colorado. This past spring, I rode my bike through the flood ravaged areas of the Front Range. Some of the paths by the river are not very scenic anymore as there are constant reminders of the devastation of the epic flood of 2013. Bridges along the bike trail are still broken and impassable. Uprooted trees dot the landscape. The ground covered in silt remains mostly barren. The results of this huge flood are still evident even a year and a half after it occurred. I paused in front of a sign that stated the high mark of the water at that particular point was fifteen feet and thought what a prime example this is, despite how ugly, of how God can and will make good things happen out of bad situations.

There is no doubt that the flood was very bad. Since I volunteered with Disaster Relief through Convoy of Hope and Samaritan's Purse just after the flood, I knew firsthand the sights and smells of devastation that a flood of that magnitude brought. Yet, I also witnessed the good in humanity as people came from all over our state and the country to help the victims. I saw volunteers unite from all walks of life with one thought in mind: to make a difference. In the field, it didn't matter if you were a big, strong oil field man or a computer geek, there was unity and work for all to do. I saw gratitude mixed with tears in the homeowners' eyes that strangers actually volunteered to wade in the sewage infested waters filled with staph and other germs on their property and stand for hours hauling bucket after bucket of muck out of their homes. The smell itself was overpowering. Time after time, I saw the disbelief in the homeowners' eyes as they questioned, "Why are you all doing this for me?"

I will be honest. I do not understand why God allows some bad things to happen yet intercedes in other situations. It seems unfair. In fact, at times, it seems like God just doesn't care. When your loved one has an affair, when you get passed over for a promotion that you know you deserve, when the life of someone you love is ended by a drunk driver, when you watch a loved one slowly die of a terminal disease, one can't help but question, "Why God? Why is this happening?" We do live in a world filled with natural disasters, suffering, and poor human choices that ricochet on others. Face it, life just isn't fair sometimes!

Even though the landscape is scarred right now from the flood, there is new growth appearing. The stems of green plants are beginning to dot the floodplains. The scars are still evident, but the land is slowly healing. Healing doesn't occur immediately; it takes time. In the future, we will only see new growth and no longer see the ruins from the flood. The landscape will look beautiful and different instead of ugly and ravaged.

The same happens in our hearts. Our scars do not heal overnight, but they will heal. It just takes time.

When we experience a flood in our lives, we wonder:

How will I ever get through this?

Will I ever love again?

Will I ever trust?

Will I ever feel happy again when right now I feel numb to the world?

A flood eventually brings about new growth. It does not happen immediately, but it will happen! Reflecting and remembering what God has done in the past for us is what gets us through the hard times. It is important to set up markers in our lives, just like the sign on the path, so that we remember what God has done for us. The sign stated that the water level's high mark was fifteen feet, but now the water is back to barely a foot deep like normal. It only stayed at the high mark for a time. Eventually, the water receded.

The Israelites knew about setting up markers to remember what God had done for them. They set up memorials built of stone so that when people walked by they could reflect and share a story of what God had done in their lives and how He had helped and delivered them. These memorials stood as a testimony of what God had done. They didn't want to forget!

Just after Samuel had prayed to God for deliverance and the Israelites defeated the attacking Philistines, Samuel set up a memorial.

"Samuel then took a large stone and placed it between the towns of Mizpah and Jeshanah. He named it Ebenezer (which means "the stone of help"), for he

said, 'Up to this point the Lord has helped us!" (1 Samuel 7:12)

Samuel set up the memorial so that the nation of Israel would not forget that God had delivered them from the Philistines. He also named the memorial "the stone of help" so that it would give them hope. Each time they looked at that memorial, they would remember how God had saved them, and they would be encouraged by the hope that God would once again be there for them during hard times.

Joshua also set up memorials to remind the people of God's love, power, mercy, and intervention. They had wandered in the wilderness for forty years because of a lack of faith and trust in God. Every time they faced a new calamity, they failed to remember what God had done for them in the past. God commanded Joshua to build a memorial so that the people would never forget how He had parted the waters of the Jordan and led them safely through.

"We will use these stones to build a memorial. In the future, your children will ask you, 'What do these stones mean?' Then you can tell them, 'They remind us that the Jordan River stopped flowing when the Ark of the Lord's Covenant went across.' These stones will stand as a memorial among the people forever." (Joshua 4: 6-7)

Biblical memorials mark pivotal moments when God was present and showed His love, power, mercy, and intervention. Do you have a memorial, a marker, in your life to remind you of what God has done? Do you have a memorial to remember the flood stage and how God eventually receded the waters? Leave reminders in your life of what God has done. Write it down in your journal! Brag about what God has done in your life and share what He has done with others. Reflect on what God has done in the past so that the next time the floods come, you will have hope for the future. Memorial stones were never private though. They were built in the open for all to see. Don't keep your memorial stone private. Be a living marker, a living testimony, of what God has done for you so that others will be encouraged and have hope as well.

When we are struggling to keep our heads above water, it is hard to praise God during a storm. However, if we choose to remember how God was there for us during our past storms, we can have hope and trust that this too shall pass. David understood this. When he was going through hard times, feeling lonely and depressed, he chose to focus on what God had done, and it gave him hope to endure and press on.

"And I said, 'This is my fate; the Most High has turned His hand against me.' But then I recall all You have done, O Lord; I remember Your wonderful deeds of long ago. They are constantly in my thoughts. I cannot stop thinking about Your mighty works." (Psalm 77:10-12)

Have you been in David's shoes and felt that God has turned against you? Has the storm you are experiencing drained and ravaged you so much that you feel that God no longer cares? Focus on your memorials. Remember what He has done for you. Trust in God's promises and have hope!

"And we know that God causes everything to work together for the good of those who love God and are called according to His purpose for them." (Romans 8:28)

Chapter 5: Spiritual Bullfighting

I love to watch rodeos and do so every opportunity I get. I enjoy the huge PRCA rodeos as well as small, local ones. There is an old western flavor to rodeos where man is pitted against beast. It reminds one of the simple days before technology invaded our lives. Rodeos bring about a comradeship among the contestants in a way that few sporting events do. My favorite event at rodeos is bull riding. In particular, I am intrigued by the bull fighters. These men sporting colorful outfits are on a mission: to protect the cowboy. They take their job very seriously.

I was a spectator at a small town rodeo this past year enjoying the bull riding as usual when I noticed an angry bull making a beeline for a cowboy that had just been bucked off. The cowboy had taken a hard fall and was slowly coming to his feet. The bull's angry eyes were focused solely on the cowboy as it ran towards him, and I held my breath in dismay. The cowboy was moving too slow from pain to get away. Just then, a bullfighter literally jumped into the bull's path, grabbed its horns and turned him away from his victim giving the cowboy time to climb the fence to safety. That bullfighter interceded for the cowboy. He risked his life to save the cowboy's life!

I don't know about you, but I don't think I am brave enough to run up to an angry bull, grab its horns, and turn its head around! Thankfully, I don't have to because I am not a bullfighter. However, I feel that there is a spiritual implication that can be drawn from this picture. Have you ever felt like you were losing a battle? Have you ever felt tossed about in the air by the enemy like the cowboy? Have you ever felt like you are lying on the ground, trying to get the energy to stand once again, and here comes the bull ready to gore you? What do you do?

A cowboy in pain is no match for an angry bull, and a broken down spirit is no match for the enemy whose sole purpose is to steal, kill, and destroy (John 10:10). When the bull attacks, do you try to be a Christian lone ranger and bear your burdens alone?

Moses knew how tiring carrying burdens by himself was, and he did not like it one bit. He complained to God.

"What did I do to deserve the burden of all these people? Did I give birth to them? Did I bring them into the world? Why did You tell me to carry them in my arms like a mother carries a nursing baby? How can I carry them to the land You swore to give their ancestors? Where am I supposed to get meat for all these people? They keep whining to me, saying, 'Give us meat to eat!' I can't carry all these people by myself! The load is far too heavy!" (Numbers 11:11-14)

God heard Moses's cry.

"Gather before Me seventy men who are recognized as elders and leaders of Israel. Bring them to the

Tabernacle to stand there with you. I will come down and talk to you there. I will take some of the Spirit that is upon you, and I will put the Spirit upon them also. They will bear the burden of the people along with you, so you will not have to carry it alone." (Numbers 11: 16-17)

God did not just provide one person to share the burden with Moses. He provided 70 men!

In the parable of the Good Samaritan, Jesus described what serving one another is like. It is not always pleasant or convenient. After a priest and a Levite both passed a wounded man on the street because they didn't want to get involved, a Samaritan came along.

"Then a despised Samaritan came along, and when he saw the man, he felt compassion for him. Going over to him, the Samaritan soothed his wounds with olive oil and wine and bandaged them. Then he put the man on his own donkey and took him to an inn where he took care of him. The next day he handed the innkeeper two silver coins telling him, 'Take care of this man. If his bill runs higher than this, I'll pay you the next time I'm here." (Luke 11:33-35)

The Good Samaritan took time out of his own busy day to fight for this man. He did not fight physically with swords or knives. However, the wounded man was in a vulnerable position. This man had been robbed, beaten, stripped of his clothes, and left half dead on the side of the road. He wasn't a pretty sight – naked and covered in blood. Yet, he needed help! He needed someone to fight for his life. He needed someone to stand between him and the darkness that was approaching. This man probably would have died had the Good Samaritan not intervened.

The Good Samaritan fought for this man by physically providing help. We can fight for each other spiritually. Scripture advises us to pray together and encourage one another.

"So encourage one another and build each other up." (1 Thessalonians 5:11)

"Let us not neglect meeting together, as some people do, but encourage one another..." (Hebrews 10:25)

"Confess your sins to each other and pray for each other so that you may be healed." (James 5:16)

"I urge you, first of all, to pray for all people. Ask God to help them; intercede on their behalf, and give thanks for them." (1 Timothy 2:1)

How can we encourage one another if we are not vulnerable with one another? It is hard to let go of pride and be truthful about what we are struggling with. However, I believe that God honors our willingness to be vulnerable. I have been in both shoes. I know what it is like to be afraid to let down my guard and admit that I am struggling. Yet, I also know that when we fight battles alone, we are like the cowboy slowly picking himself up off the ground - shaken, battered, and bruised. We stare in alarm at the enemy coming to attack once more knowing that we don't have the strength to fight. That cowboy had a bullfighter to intercede for him. That bullfighter saw his vulnerable condition and rushed in to help.

We can do the same! We can spiritually fight for each other in prayer! We can encourage one another to stand up once again and face another day because the storm is not going to last forever. We can give hope to those who have lost it. The only way for this to truly be effective is if you are willing to be vulnerable and say, "Hey, I'm really struggling. Could you pray for me? Could you fight for me?"

Fighting for one another involves vulnerability. It involves us stripping our pride just as the wounded man in the parable of the Good Samaritan was stripped of his clothes. Spiritual fighting does not involve physical wounds, but it takes willingness to show our emotional wounds. It requires being humble and saying, "I need help." Compassion and patience are needed on the bullfighter's part. Spiritual fighting is not always pleasant or convenient. Yet, the Bible advises us over and over to pray together, intercede for one another, and encourage one another.

Are you ready for battle? The Bible says in Ephesians 6:12,

"For we are not fighting against flesh and blood enemies, but against rulers and authorities of the unseen world, against mighty powers in this dark world, and against evil spirits in the heavenly places."

Do you have the courage to be vulnerable with one another and the willingness to get involved? There is power in praying together!

"For where two or three are gathered together as My followers, I am there among them." (Matthew 18:20)

Are you ready to pray, intercede, and encourage those who are fighting a battle? Are you willing to be vulnerable and ask for prayer? Are you willing to be a spiritual bullfighter?

Chapter 6: Lessons from a Train Ride

Once a month, I have a "special day" with each of the boys I nanny. They really look forward to their "special days" in which one of them gets to choose an activity and enjoy being the center of attention with one-on-one time. Earlier this summer, Matt, four and half years old, chose fishing for his "special day". I'm not wild about fishing, and worms really gross me out. I'm thankful to report that he has learned to bait his own hook this summer! I shared his excitement as he caught multiple small fish and tried to hide my disgust as I removed one after another off his hook. Even with gloves on, I still don't like handling them! After a few hours, we decided to take a break and ride a train that loops around a short area of the park.

Since I have always ridden the train with the boys, I bought our tickets like normal. We each held a ticket as we waited in line to board the small train. As I gave my ticket to the conductor and began to follow Matt into the freight car he chose, he suddenly pushed me backwards.

"I don't want you to ride with me. I want to ride by myself!" he declared.

I began to board anyway but stopped when he

pushed me once again.

"I want to be treated like a big boy. Go away! I want to ride by myself!" he demanded.

I felt hurt that he didn't want me to ride with him. This was our "special day"! I look forward to them just as much as the boys do! However, I decided to honor his wishes to ride by himself since he is almost five years old. I knew that he was just exerting his independence because he saw other boys his age riding alone without a grownup. I sat on the hard, wooden bench at the train station and waited for the train to make its slow loop. His attitude had hurt me, and I pouted as I waited.

I began to think of how often I had the very same attitude with God. How many times have I wanted to spend time with God when it was convenient for me? How many times have I been okay with hanging out with God when nobody's around but embarrassed to have my peers see me doing so? How many times have I wanted to exert my independence from God? How many times have I told God, "I want to do this by myself! I want to be treated like a big girl!"?

A few years ago, I was exerting my own independence and doing the very same thing with God that Matt did to me about the train ride. "I will spend time with You here, but not here. I want to do this one on my own all by myself! I want everyone to see how big I am!" God, in His wisdom, let this strong-willed girl have her independence. My demand led me straight to a spiritual wilderness because we cannot put more stock into depending on ourselves and our own abilities than on God and His abilities. When we try to live independently from God, we end up in a wilderness apart from God. In the wilderness, however, is where we learn and are reminded that we cannot make it alone. We need God! We need His companionship, His love, His mercy, and His peace.

Sometimes God leads us into the wilderness to teach us a lesson. Many people believe that God sends us to the wilderness as punishment, and sometimes that may be, but He also sends us to the wilderness to strengthen our faith. Our entry into the wilderness does not always make sense to us. The Israelites experienced that in their journey to the Promised Land.

"When Pharaoh finally let the people go, God did not lead them along the main road that runs through Philistine territory, even though that was the shortest route to the Promised Land. God said, 'If the people are faced with a battle, they might change their minds and return to Egypt.' So God led them in a roundabout way through the wilderness toward the Red Sea." (Exodus 13: 17-18)

God led the Israelites to the wilderness because He knew that their faith was fickle. We see in further chapters in Exodus where the Israelites were longing to return to Egypt.

"Why did you bring us out here to die in the wilderness? Weren't there enough graves for us in Egypt? What have you done to us? Why did you make us leave Egypt?" (Exodus 14: 11)

Sound familiar? How about when the Israelites were glorifying their past and not remembering the hardships that occurred?

"If only the Lord had killed us back in Egypt,' they moaned. 'There we sat around pots filled with meat and ate all the bread we wanted. But now you have brought us into this wilderness to starve us all to death." (Exodus 16:3)

How quickly they seem to have forgotten their years of slavery!

"So the Egyptians made the Israelites their slaves. They appointed brutal slave drivers over them, hoping to wear them down with crushing labor. ...So the Egyptians worked the people of Israel without mercy. They made their lives bitter, forcing them to mix mortar and make bricks and do all the work in the fields. They were ruthless in all their demands." (Exodus 1:11-14)

Hmm, crushing labor and ruthless demands! That doesn't sound like the wonderful life they were remembering back in Egypt and longing for again. In the wilderness, when things were not going as they would have liked, they quickly forgot their heartfelt pleas to God while under the yoke of slavery.

"But the Israelites continued to groan under their burden of slavery. They cried out for help, and their cry rose up to God." (Exodus 2:23)

The Israelites wanted deliverance from slavery. When they got their independence, it wasn't what they imagined it would be like. Instead of taking a direct route into the Promised Land, God led them through the wilderness. It wasn't the easy life they were expecting. It was hard, hot, and tiring. Over and over, they complained to God and proved their unfaithfulness. God's plan was not to get the Israelites to the Promised Land by the fastest route possible. His plan was for the people to know Him, love Him, serve Him, and experience Him.

"This is what the Lord of Heaven's Armies, the God of Israel, says: 'Take your burnt offering and your other sacrifices and eat them yourselves! When I led your ancestors out of Egypt, it was not burnt offerings and sacrifices that I wanted from them. This is what I told them: 'Obey Me, and I will be your God, and you will be My people." (Jeremiah 7: 21-22)

"What makes you think I want all your sacrifices?...Learn to do good. Seek justice. Help the oppressed. Defend the cause of the orphans. Fight for the rights of widows." (Isaiah 1:11-17)

"These people say they are Mine. They honor Me with their lips, but their hearts are far from Me. And their worship of Me is nothing but man-made rules learned by rote." (Isaiah 29:13)

There is more to obedience that ritualistic observing of religious practices. True obedience involves the heart.

"You must love the Lord your God with all your heart, all your soul, and all your strength. And you must commit yourselves wholeheartedly to these commands that I am giving you today. Repeat them again and again to your children. Talk about them when you are at home and when you are on the road, when you are going to bed and when you are getting up. Tie them to your hands and wear them on your forehead as reminders. Write them on the doorposts of your house and on your gates." (Deuteronomy 6: 5-9)

"You must love the Lord your God with all your

heart, all your soul, and all your mind. This is the first and greatest commandment. A second is equally important: 'Love your neighbor as yourself.' The entire law and all the demands of the prophets are based on these two commandments." (Matthew 22:37-39)

We want to please those we love. Obeying God is no different. When we choose to follow and obey God out of love, it makes us joyous because it comes from the heart. If you are just going to church and mouthing the words to the songs because you feel that is what you have to do or that it might get you points with God, your actions are in vain. He wants you to worship Him from your heart. He wants your love. When you do love Him and worship Him from your heart, it shows in your life and changes everything you do and who you are. You have the desire to "*Learn to do good. Seek justice. Help the oppressed. Defend the cause of the orphans. Fight for the rights of widows" (Exodus 1:17)*. You do this not because you feel obligated to help but because you are filled with God's compassion for others. Love for God changes everything about you!

God wanted the Israelites to know Him and to experience Him. He wanted them to trust Him in every situation. He wanted their hearts! He knew they were torn between Him and the pagan gods of the Egyptians. He wanted their faithfulness, so He led them into the wilderness to teach them.

The wilderness is not easy. Sometimes, it is a long, hard, frustrating journey. We feel deserted and depressed. Nobody seems to understand what we are going through. God seems distant and absent. We feel alone, hopeless, and abandoned! Our faith wavers. Doubts creep in:

"Has God forgotten me? Does He still care about me? Why did He bring me into the wilderness? Doesn't He love me?"

Our mind deceives us into longing for the good old days. Are we really that different from the Israelites? Don't we spend our days in the wilderness in self-pity asking, "Why me?"

Sometimes what we need most in the wilderness is a change of heart. In wilderness times, it is easy to picture God as aloof, cruel, and uncaring. It is easy to become filled with anger, bitterness, and self-pity over our circumstances. We need to learn to rejoice in the storms! We don't rejoice at the storms when lightening is striking us with problem after problem because we enjoy the pain and hurt. Rather, we rejoice in the storms because we know the storm is not going to last forever, and this journey will eventually end. We can rejoice because we remember what God has done for us in the past, and we have hope for the future.

"For I know the plans I have for you,' declares the Lord. 'They are plans for good and not for disaster, to give you a future and, a hope." (Jeremiah 29:11)

I will admit that I don't enjoy trials and hardships. I don't enjoy God proving to me that my faith in Him is as wavering as a ship lost in a storm at sea. However, I have learned to view wilderness experiences as an opportunity for growth as James advises.

"When troubles come your way, consider it an opportunity for great joy. For you know that when your faith is tested, your endurance has a chance to grow. So let it grow, for when your endurance is fully developed,

you will be perfect and complete, needing nothing." (James 1:2-4)

Matt did not have the same huge smile on his face when the train arrived back at the station as he did when it departed. It turned out that he didn't really enjoy riding by himself as much as he thought he would. That seven minute train ride felt like a long, lonely journey to him. He missed his friend! He found out that it's not much fun to have a "special day" when you are all by yourself on a train ride. It's not much fun to live without God either! It is lonely without His constant companionship. I praise God for those lonely times of spiritual wilderness because it is in those times that I realize just how much I need God in my life. I realize in those wilderness periods that I truly cannot make it on my own without Him. The ending result is that I draw closer to Him.

Are you wandering in the wilderness? Are you crying, "Why me?", as you complain that your circumstances are overwhelming and God must have abandoned you? Humble yourself and draw near to God (James 4:7-8). Your circumstances might not change, but your attitude will! You will have hope and strength to face tomorrow. Trust that God will see you through.

> *"If we are unfaithful, He remains faithful, for He cannot deny who He is." (2 Timothy 2:13)*

(Reflections in the wilderness)

Chapter 7: Settling at Good Enough

I put Matt and Sam on the climbing wall on a regular basis this summer. The wall is about twenty-five feet high which to Matt, at four and half years old, must seem like Mt. Everest. I enjoyed watching Matt slowly gain confidence as he climbed higher and higher each week - until he got halfway. He was very proud of reaching the midway point. Each time Matt got about twelve feet off the ground, he gripped his handhold tightly as he paused and turned to see if I was watching and shouted, "Look at me!" I praised him and enveloped him in hugs every time the automatic belay set him safely back on the ground. Climbing twelve feet is quite an accomplishment for his age! Matt decided halfway was as far as he could go. The next thirteen feet seemed like an impossibility for him, so he stopped midway for several weeks.

I encouraged Matt each week to climb a little higher and gave him pointers on where to put his hands and feet. Each time, he replied, "It's too high. This is as far as I can go!" He was too scared to climb higher even though I kept telling him over and over, "I know you can do it; I believe in you!" He had settled for the midway point. It was good enough for him. He felt safe there. I knew that he could make it all the way to the top if he just tried, but he didn't have that same confidence in himself.

After a few weeks of stalling at the midway point, he took a hesitating step upward. As he reached his arm up to grab the next handhold, he hesitated too long and the automatic belay gently lowered him to the ground. The problem with an automatic belay is that it allows for no hesitancy. There is no taking a break on an automatically belayed rope as one can when a person is doing the belaying. "Did you see me?" he asked with a smile as I gave him a huge hug and told him how proud I was of him. I showed him the video I had taken of him climbing a step higher than he had ever done before. "Look! I told you that you can do it! Way to go! That was awesome!" I praised him. He smiled widely as he was very proud of himself.

Matt got back on the climbing wall a week later. I expected him to maybe move a step higher than the last time since he had finally gotten the confidence to climb above the midway point he had been stalling at. To my surprise, he reached the midway point with no hesitation and kept going higher and higher. He climbed until he was less than a foot from the top! I erupted in cheers! He reached for the gong that is hanging at the top to ring the bell, lost his grip, and down he went. The automatic belay allows no hesitation. I personally find it harder than climbing with a belay partner. "Wow! Way to go! You almost made it!" I cheered as I rushed to hug him. He replied, "I didn't ring the bell though". Finally having gotten his confidence, he got right back on the wall and tried again.

Matt climbed just about to the top again, reached

for the gong, lost his hand grip, and belayed down six more times in a row. He was determined to go all the way and not settle for "just about to the top". He tried and tried until his arms wore out and no longer had the strength to climb. As he removed his climbing harness he told me, "I'm going to ring it next time!" He sure did!

It is a major accomplishment for a four and half year old to climb to the top of a twenty-five foot rock wall. In his eyes, it probably seemed as impossible as climbing Mount Everest does to most of us! Yet, the lesson he is learning is that nothing is truly impossible with God! He is learning that he can do all things through Christ who gives him strength! He is learning not to settle for halfway but to go all the way! Matt is learning through climbing not to give up even when he thinks he is too little or not strong enough. Climbing is teaching him that what he thinks is impossible and too huge can actually be possible. One of the reasons he is learning this is because of my constant encouragement as he hears me repetitively say, "You can do this! I believe in you!"

When the Israelites first reached the outskirts of the Promised Land, Moses, who was chronically lacking in faith, sent out a group of men to explore it. He wanted to know who inhabited it and what they were like before he entered. When the group of men returned after exploring the land for forty days, they brought back conflicting reports.

"We entered the land you sent us to explore, and it is indeed a bountiful country – a land flowing with milk and honey. " (Numbers 13:27)

"We can't go up against them! They are stronger

than we are!" (Numbers 13:31)

"The land we traveled through and explored will devour anyone who goes to live there. All the people we saw were huge. We even saw giants there, the descendants of Anak. Next to them we felt like grasshoppers, and that's what they thought too." (Numbers: 13:31-33)

Caleb believed that all things were possible with God and had a different take. Caleb knew that God was bigger than the circumstances.

*"Let's go at once to take the land,' he said. 'We can certainly conquer it!" (Numbers 13:3*0)

We have a tendency to exaggerate our fears. How does a report that starts off by proving God's faithfulness to His promise to send them to a land filled with milk and honey become "They are stronger than we are!" and lead to "Next to them we felt like grasshoppers"? I love how they added, "and that's what they thought too". Did they have the gall to ask the giants what they thought of them? "Umm, excuse me Mr. Giant, but do you think we stand a chance against you?" The more we focus on our fears, the more impossible and hopeless a situation seems. God became angry at their lack of faith in Him. He sentenced all but Caleb and Joshua to wander in the wilderness for forty years and to never experience living in the Promised Land. The faithlessness of the Israelites caused them to miss out on God's promise for them.

After forty years of wandering in the wilderness, Moses and all of the people who had been twenty years or older at the door of the Promised Land had died except for Caleb and Joshua. God then chose Joshua to lead the people. As soon as Joshua was chosen, he didn't hesitate. Instead of sending twelve men for forty days to scout it out, Joshua sent two men as spies for a few days into Jericho to plan an attack. Upon their return, Joshua led all of the Israelites to the banks of the Jordan River where they camped for three days. The Jordan River was overflowing and looked impossible. However, Joshua wasn't filled with fears of how they would cross. He believed God's promise!

"The time has come for you to lead these people, the Israelites, across the Jordan River into the land I am giving them. I promise you what I promised Moses: 'Wherever you set foot, you will be on land I have given you'...No one will be able to stand against you as long as you live. For I will be with you as I was with Moses. I will not fail you or abandon you...

Study this Book of Instruction continually. Mediate on it day and night so you will be sure to obey everything written in it. Only then will you prosper and succeed in all you do. This is My command – 'be strong and courageous! Do not be afraid or discouraged. For the Lord your God is with you wherever you go." (Joshua 1: 2-9)

God had told Joshua to lead the people across the Jordan River. Despite the circumstances of the raging water, Joshua chose to obey. He believed His God would make the impossible possible. For three days, the people waited as they stared at the impossible looking obstacle in front of them. They had grown up hearing of the Israelites' miraculous escape from the Egyptians. They had heard the stories of how God parted the waters of the Red Sea. Yet, surely they must have wondered, "Would God do it again?"

The longer we stare at an obstacle, the more fearful we become. Surely the people had doubts not only about the river crossing but about what waited for them on the other side. It would be safer to settle right where they were. Having a view of the Promised Land was good enough, right? I enjoy climbing 14ers (mountains over 14,000 feet). I can tell you with all honesty that having a view of the mountain and standing on top of the mountain are two very separate feelings and experiences. It's not enough for me to view it. I need to experience it even though I know that there are dangers lurking.

Joshua may not have known just how he was going to lead two million people across a raging river, but He chose to believe God's promise and command to be with him as he did so. Joshua refused to settle because God had given him clear instructions. He trusted God's word. At that time, the Ark of the Covenant represented God's presence. Joshua told the Levite priests who were carrying it to lead the way and for the people to follow. In other words, he said, "Follow God!" As soon as the priests stepped into the water, it began backing up until the riverbed was dry. Scripture says that it backed up "a great distance away" (Joshua 3:16) It took some time for the Jordan riverbed to become passable. Sometimes we have obstacles in our lives that we want God to immediately fix. It's important to remember that He is orchestrating events even when we can't see it. Sometimes, it just takes time to see the outcome.

We all need encouragement and reminders in our lives that even when something seems impossible, nothing is truly impossible with God! I could have let

Matt settle for midway, and that alone would have been a huge accomplishment for a 4 year old. But, I knew he could make it to the top. Maybe you are reading this right now, and you feel like Matt did. You are stalling and hanging out at the midway point. You are halfway there, and you have given up. You have settled for "good enough". Sure you made an accomplishment going halfway, but you aren't as far as you could be. You are stalled at the midway point thinking, "That is all I can do. I'm too shy, too weak, too young, too old, too tired, too washed up, too broken, too useless, too lonely!" God doesn't want us to settle out of fear when He will give us the strength to face our challenges.

I wonder who in your life needs that same encouragement. Who do you know facing insurmountable odds? Who is contemplating starting a business yet settling for being an employee because the undertaking seems so impossible that they have given up on achieving their dreams? They just don't think they can. They don't think they are strong enough. Who is fighting a disease that seems impossible to beat? Instead of continuing to fight, they are settling for that doctor's diagnosis instead of seeking second, third, and fourth opinions along with alternative treatments. Who is elderly and has settled for a life of watching television day after day because they feel like they no longer have anything to contribute? All they really need is just some encouragement to feel worthy and needed once again. They need someone to help them get involved in something. Who do you know who has a dream that seems impossible to achieve and just needs someone to believe in them? Who do you know who may be a caregiver for a spouse or disabled child? Who is struggling to get through the day and needs encouragement to keep going? It might be a friend, a co-worker, a neighbor, or even yourself.

I can honestly say that I never would have started a photography business if it hadn't been for people who encouraged me. I lacked the confidence that people would actually buy my work. I didn't believe that I was "good enough". I was too afraid of rejection to even get started. I had settled for a life of taking photos and sharing them among friends instead of starting a photography business for profit. The only reason I started a business was because of friends who believed in me. These friends believed in me so much that they went so far as to set up my first showings for me. They had the confidence in me that I lacked. I also never would have gone into public speaking had Josh not believed in me. His encouragement gave me the confidence to speak in front of a congregation of three hundred people at his church despite the fact that I was extremely shy, insecure, terrified of rejection, and struggled with social anxiety at that time.

I want to remind you that nothing is impossible with God (Luke 1:37) and that you truly can do all things through Christ who gives you strength! Take one step of faith into the waters of the Jordan River, then another. Even if you feel like you are all alone and that nobody truly believes in you, trust that God does. He is your number one supporter! He is on your side! Every step of faith you take, He cheers! I could not wait to brag on Matt's accomplishment on the climbing wall. If I can get so excited over the accomplishments of a child who is not even mine, think of how excited God feels about His children!

"This is My command – 'be strong and courageous! Do not be afraid or discouraged. For the Lord your God is with you wherever you go." *(Joshua 1: 2-9)*

Chapter 8: Fickle Behavior

Three year olds make confusing statements.

"I want you!"

"I don't want you!"

"I need you!"

"I don't need you!"

"Stay with me!"

"Go away!"

"I do it myself!"

The three year old boy that I nanny, Sam, says these words on a regular basis, sometimes within minutes of each other! He tries to exert his independence, yet the minute I give him exactly what he is wishing for, he wants the opposite. It is frustrating to say the least! After a trying morning with Sam, I gave myself a time-out in the bathroom while God gave me a spiritual lesson with Sam's words.

How many times have I said the very same things to God?

"God, I want you in my life in everything I do."

"Actually, God, I'm mad at You, so I don't want You right now!"

"God, I need You!"

"Well, actually God, I don't need You after all. I've got everything under control."

"God, stay with me!"

"Actually God, I'm mad at You! Just go away and leave me alone!"

"You know what God, I want to do this by myself! "

Hmm, there's not a lot of difference in Sam's words to me versus my words to God. I think if you are perfectly honest, there's probably not a lot of difference in your words to God either. Why is that? Most of us wouldn't talk to a friend like that, but when it comes to God, we behave like a three year old. When He doesn't work things out the way we wanted them to be worked out, we get angry at Him and no longer want Him around. We don't have a physical door to slam, but we slam the door to our hearts as loudly as we can. We want God to know that we are mad at Him.

Just like the three year old, we want our independence, but seeking independence from God is not the solution. That only produces disaster. Yet, time after time, we tell Him, "I've got this part of my life under control. I don't need You right now."

We look down our noses at the Biblical characters, especially the Israelites when they were on their journey to the Promised Land. That entire journey was filled with the people's fickle attitudes. In chapter 15 of Exodus, they were praising God for delivering them from Egypt. In the very next chapter, they were longing to return to Egypt. In chapter 24, they promised to do everything that God had commanded. However, by chapter 32, they no longer trusted God to lead them out of Egypt and instead built a golden calf to worship and lead them. This was typical behavior from people who were really no different than us.

Throughout the Bible, we see examples of this. Jesus experienced the people's fickleness firsthand. Consider Luke 4. When Jesus returned to his childhood home of Nazareth, he went to the synagogue on the Sabbath and began to read Isaiah 61:1-2 aloud.

"The Spirit of the Lord is upon Me, for He has anointed Me to bring Good News to the poor. He has sent Me to proclaim that captives will be released, that the blind will see, that the oppressed will be set free, and that the time of the Lord's favor has come."

Every eye in the synagogue was focused on Him as He then proclaimed, *"The Scripture you've just heard has been fulfilled this very day!"*

At first, the people stared at Jesus in amazement. Nazareth was His hometown! They had watched him grow up. They murmured among themselves as they praised Him. The people had heard rumors of the miracles Jesus had performed in nearby towns. They were proud of Him. If billboards had existed back in their time, they would have erected a large one that said, "Home of Jesus Christ the Miracle Worker!" In their hearts, they were considering the tourism that could be brought to Nazareth, the trinkets to be sold, and the money to be made.

Jesus knew their hearts and their true intentions which is why He stated,

"You will undoubtedly quote Me this proverb: 'Physician, heal yourself' – meaning, 'Do miracles here in Your hometown like those You did in Capernaum." (Luke 4:23)

Jesus knew that the people really just wanted to be entertained. They wanted to capitalize off of his supernatural powers. They didn't really care or want to know how the Scriptures were being fulfilled in their presence nor were they seeking to be in the presence of the Lord. They just wanted to see for themselves the miracles that they had heard rumors of. They were excited not for Him but for the magic show they were sure He was going to perform for them. After all, He was a hometown boy. Surely, He would give them the best show of all!

Even though Jesus knew their hearts, He continued to speak truth to them.

"But I tell you the truth, no prophet is accepted in His own hometown." (Luke 4:24)

Jesus then gave the people a lesson of repentance, knowing that they would stop praising Him and that they would want Him out of their sight.

"Certainly there were many needy widows in Israel in Elijah's time, when the heavens were closed for three and a half years, and a severe famine devastated the land. Yet Elijah was not sent to any of them. He was sent instead to a foreigner – a widow of Zarephath in the

land of Sidon. And there were many lepers in Israel in the time of the prophet, Elijah, but the only one healed was Naaman, a Syrian." (Luke 4:25-27)

Jesus tried to make the people understand that God considered these foreigners more righteous and deserving of His help than the Israelites at the time because of their sinful nature and the way they had hardened their hearts against Him. Jesus gave these examples as a cry of repentance to the people. He was telling them to be less concerned about entertainment and more concerned about spiritual truths. Jesus knew that the people in his hometown just wanted to see Him cast out demons and heal the blind. They weren't interested in changing their hearts. Their response proved it.

"When they heard this, the people in the synagogue were furious. Jumping up, they mobbed Him and forced Him to the edge of the hill on which the town was built. They intended to push Him over the cliff, but He passed right through the crowd and went on His way." (Luke 4:28-30)

If Jesus wasn't going to perform for the people the way that they wanted Him to, they didn't want Him around. They were so angry at Jesus that they were willing to push Him over the cliff. They had put Jesus in a box. They had expectations of Him. He was their hometown hero. They felt that they deserved an even grander show of healings and casting out of demons than the nearby towns. Instead of an entertaining performance, all they got was a message to repent. They were furious!

How did the people of Nazareth go from praising

Jesus for His miracles to wanting to kill Him in such a short period of time? How could the people praise Jesus as He made His triumphant entry on a donkey to Jerusalem (Luke 19:37) then later shout, "Crucify Him" (Luke 23:21)? People are fickle! It is easy to proclaim that we want God in our lives, but the truth is that we don't always want to listen to what He is teaching us. We want to be entertained. We want to be part of His miraculous works, yet when He chooses not to do what we expected of Him, we get angry. We no longer want anything to do with Him.

The people of Nazareth were so angry, in fact, that they missed a miracle that Jesus did right in front of them. He passed through the crowd. This angry mob that wanted to end his life didn't even notice when Jesus passed right through them and went on His way. Sometimes miracles don't come as dramatically as we expect them to.

It is hard to acknowledge that most of us behave like a three year old in our relationship with God. Why do we do that? We put God in a box and expect Him to perform to our expectations, and when He doesn't, we feel let down. We feel angry and upset. We somehow feel that we as the created know more than the Creator. I like to think at this point in my spiritual journey that I behave more as a teenager with God than a three year old. I have fewer tantrums and a little more understanding that His ways are not my own. Yet, just the other day, I was angry at Him and slamming the doors to my heart once more. My mom is rapidly degenerating from vascular dementia, and I struggle with questions of how a loving God could allow someone who loves Him to suffer through that. Why?

The pat answers we give each other when going through hard times such as: “God works everything for the good of those who love Him. God has plans for good and not evil, to give you a future and a hope” are not what we want to hear when news of genocide flashes on our televisions, cancer strikes a friend, and a loved one slowly wastes away. It’s hard to see God’s goodness in the face of so much suffering. It is tough to wonder why He allows things to happen that, if we were God, we know we wouldn’t allow. So, we do the only thing we know to do. We yell at Him as we slam the door to our hearts. In our minds, God let us down, so we give up on Him. “Leave me alone!” we demand.

Some of us open up the door to our hearts again and lean on God once more. Others turn away from Him forever, angry because they feel let down. They argue over and over that God doesn’t exist and that He can’t exist, when in truth, they are just mad at Him. Did they know the true and living God? Or, did they worship a version of God that they built in their heads? A man-made god will always fail you.

Sometimes Bible promises do seem like pat answers, yet that is where faith comes in. Yes, I run to my room and slam the door to my heart at times when I get overwhelmed by the suffering I see. I can’t understand why God allows children to starve, babies to die, and women to be tortured in the Sudan. I can’t understand why God allows people to slowly waste away from cancer and lose their brain and physical functions due to dementia. It doesn’t seem fair. However, even though I can’t understand God’s purposes in not intervening, I do know one thing. God is love! The truth about God’s love is not that He allows bad things to happen; rather it is His promise that when they do, He will be right there beside you, walking with you, every step of the way. He cries when you cry. He is waiting for you to lean on His shoulder. He is standing there with arms open wide ready to hug you and comfort you.

I have a note on my desk that simply says, "Praise God in the storm!" This doesn't mean to praise God because of circumstances. It means to praise God in spite of circumstances! When you don't understand something God is allowing, praise Him for His attributes. Praise Him for His character. Praise Him for what you know to be true about Him. Praise God for what He has done in the past in your life. That is what gets me through the storms. Praising God is what gets me through the hard times and the doubts and fears that come with them. We may not understand what God is doing, but we can trust that He knows more than we do.

As we learn to praise God in the storms and see the blessings that He brings about in the midst of them no matter how small, we grow spiritually in our relationship with God. We are less inclined to scream, "Go away!" and more inclined to cry, "Draw nearer!" God is the best Friend we can ever have. Even though we know He has the power to change things, we need to accept it when He chooses not to and trust that He has a plan with a better purpose in mind that we may not see. We don't blame our friends for the problems of this world, and we shouldn't blame God. He just wants to be our Friend. Just like we run to our friends for advice and comfort, He wants us to run to Him. He wants us to have hope for the future because of what He has done for us in the past. Peace in the storm means comfort, love, and hope.

My question to you today is how would you rate your behavior with God? Have you given up on Him completely? Have you demanded Him to go away because you feel let down? Do you act like a three year old with Him alternating between "I want You; I don't want You. I need You; I don't need You." Is your relationship with God based on your circumstances? Or, do you have a relationship with God despite your circumstances? Have you put God in a box? Are you worshiping your image of Him? Or, are you worshiping God for who He is, not for who you want Him to be? The only relationship that will truly last is one in which you can praise Him in the storms despite your circumstances.

"Love the Lord your God with all your heart, all your soul, all your strength, and all your mind." (Luke 10:27)

Chapter 9: Acceptance

Two dogs live upstairs from me. From the time that they were wee pups, I didn't like them. It wasn't that they did anything specifically to me. I didn't trust them solely on the basis of their breed's reputation. Max and Bella are Dobermans. I have been slightly afraid of Dobermans ever since I was a young child.

I grew up in a very rural community where there was an old fashioned country store at a three way stop. I loved it when my mom sent me on an errand to that country store to buy potato chips for lunch. I happily hopped on my red Schwinn bike with the white basket decorated in flowers and began to pedal up the long, steep hill toward the country store. Just as I topped the hill and had the store in sight, my heart pounded in anguish each time. Two Dobermans lived at a home just before the three way stop. These were two very aggressive Dobermans who delighted in snarling and charging at my bicycle as I pedaled along. The dogs were never tied up. As a young child, I was terrified of them.

When the family who lives above me got Max and Bella as puppies, I didn't want anything to do with them. Sure, they looked cute and innocent as puppies, but I knew just what Dobermans were capable of and didn't trust them one bit. As they began to grow and were allowed outside, I passed them by, as aloof as I could be. I didn't spend any time petting them. After all, I didn't want to lose my hand or any other essential body part. I honestly never gave these dogs a chance simply because I had a bad experience with those other Dobermans as a child. I judged Max and Bella based on their reputation and based on my past experiences with their breed.

I would have been happy to continue to ignore the dogs except that Max decided that he was going to win me over. He began running to my SUV when I came home and laid his head on my lap as soon as I opened up my door. Then, he pressed his head harder and harder on me until I finally petted him. In fact, he wouldn't walk away to allow me to get out my SUV until I petted him. I feared upsetting him, so I did just what he wanted. Then, he began to greet me anytime he saw me by pressing his body against mine while looking up at me with soulful eyes until I tentatively petted him. This process went on for several months, and slowly I began to see his heart and not his breed when I looked at him.

While Max was attempting to win me over, Bella was quite content to stay aloof. After all, I had given her no attention, why should she give me any? But, after watching her brother finally getting the attention from me that he craved so much, she began to try as well. Soon, she joined her brother to greet me when I opened up my SUV door. Bella doesn't have the same outgoing personality that her brother does, however, and she doesn't completely trust me. She will only approach me if Max does. If I reach out a hand to pet her without her brother around, she backs away quickly. We are still a little unsure of each other.

I was recently thinking of the different personalities of these two dogs. As I reflected how Max persistently chipped away at the reserved walls of my heart in his attempt to get me to like him, I suddenly realized that my experiences with people have been very similar to my experiences with these dogs. Maybe you can relate.

How many times have you judged people simply because of their reputation without even taking the time to get to know them? How often have you avoided a person because of their past without realizing just how much people can change? When have you judged someone of a certain color or nationality simply because you had a bad experience with another person of their race? How many times have you not taken the time to get to know a person's heart because of preconceived notions about them? Has someone like Max practically begged to be your friend, yet you were too scared of being hurt to give that person a chance?

Joshua 2 tells the story of Rahab. She was a temple prostitute who lived in the walled city of Jericho. As her clients came and went, Rahab heard stories of the God of the Israelites. She wondered about a God who had parted the Red Sea for His people and delivered them from slavery in Egypt. This God seemed alive and real to His people, not aloof and made of stone like the ones she worshipped. Rahab desired to know this God, but questioned whether this God would desire to know her, a temple prostitute. After all, she wasn't exactly accepted by society.

Rahab believed so much in this God that she had never seen and had only heard stories of that she hid two spies from the Israelite camp on her roof. Rahab had the opportunity to betray the two spies into the hands of her people. Instead, she helped them escape because she believed that their God would conquer the land. In return, she asked for their promise that she and her family would be spared when Jericho was conquered. The men promised to spare their lives if she left a scarlet rope hanging from her window as a sign to the Israelites. The two spies kept their promise and moved her family to a safe place in the Israelite camp during the battle.

Rahab was spared because of her faith and given a new life with the Israelites. The Bible is not clear whether they fully accepted her or shunned her for her past. However, it does state that she became a part of the lineage of Jesus. Regardless of whether the people accepted her or not, God did! He knew her heart!

The Bible is not shy about Rahab's past. She is called, "Rahab the prostitute", five times in the Bible. Her reputation followed her for life. Yet, the Bible mentions Rahab as a hero of faith in Hebrews 11:31.

"It was by faith that Rahab the prostitute was not destroyed with the people in her city who refused to obey God. For she had given a friendly welcome to the spies."

How was a prostitute mentioned in the same Hall of Faith as Noah, Abraham, Isaac, Jacob, Moses, Gideon, Samson, David, and Samuel? Rahab's name is listed among the heroes of the Old Testament! The Bible doesn't cover up her past, but it does show that she became a woman of great faith through the grace of God. God accepted her! I believe that God always included the description of Rahab's past to show the hurting, wounded, and broken of this world that there is hope. Even though Rahab was a prostitute, she wasn't too messed up for God to save and change.

Rahab's occupation as a prostitute represented sin. The scarlet rope she hung from her window illustrated salvation through the blood of Christ. Despite what you may have done or where you are in life, you are not too messed up for God. Rahab's story proves that! Rahab was still a prostitute when God delivered her from Jericho. She did not have to get cleaned up for God. He accepted her just as she was because of her faith in Him. Rahab's messy past became her greatest story of what God had done in her life!

What are you judging others for doing? The spies could have self-righteously looked at Rahab in disgust despite her good deeds and refused to honor her request for deliverance. However, they chose to show her mercy and even offered their own lives as a guarantee for her safety.

Max taught me an important life lesson about getting to know someone's heart before I form an opinion about them. It is hard to set aside preconceived notions about people. Yet, it is imperative when one realizes just how many people out there are longing for love and acceptance and need to know that they are not too messed up for God. What are you ashamed of about your life? Who are you judging and afraid to accept? If God can accept Rahab, mistakes and all, surely we should be able to accept one another.

"Teacher, which is the most important commandment in the law of Moses?'

Jesus replied, 'You must love the Lord your God with all your heart, all your soul, and all your mind. This is the first and greatest commandment. A second is equally important: 'Love your neighbor as yourself.' The entire law and all of the demands of the prophets are based on these two commandments."

(Matthew 22:36-40)

Chapter 10: The Blame Game

When Matt was three years old, he was particularly challenging one day and spit a mouthful of his milk into his younger brother's face. I sent Matt to his room and advised him to have a talk with Jesus about his attitude while he was in there. Hearing Matt talking a few minutes later, I walked to the door of his room and eavesdropped on his prayer.

"Jesus, it so much fun to spit milk in Sam's face. But, Tonya makes a mean face at me when I do that, and I don't want to go to time out anymore. Can you please make Tonya not make mean faces at me and give her a new attitude? Amen!"

I quickly stepped into the bathroom and burst into laughter at his prayer. A few minutes later, Matt excitedly ran into the living room with a huge smile.

"Guess what! Jesus said He will give you a new attitude!" he declared.

"Why me?" I questioned.

"Because I want to spit milk in Sam's face again. It's

so-oo much fun!" Matt explained.

Matt did what most of us have done at some point in our lives. He prayed for my attitude to be changed instead of his own. Matt did not see his behavior as the problem, nor did he want to change it. He simply prayed for my attitude and reaction to him to change. Are you guilty of doing that? I know I am. I have prayed for other people's attitudes to change, never realizing that mine was the problem and not theirs.

King David made a series of mistakes. At a time when kings normally went to war, David sent his commander, Joab, to fight in his place and stayed behind in Jerusalem. While David was lounging around on the roof of his palace, he noticed a beautiful woman taking a bath. David loved women and sent someone to find out who she was. He was informed that the woman's name was Bathsheba and that she was the wife of Uriah the Hittite. Even though David knew that she was married, he sent servants to bring her to the palace and then had sex with her. When Bathsheba realized she was pregnant, she sent David a message to let him know.

David quickly devised a plan to cover up his actions. He sent word to Joab to send Uriah to the palace. David questioned Uriah about the war when he arrived and then ordered Uriah to go home and relax. David was hoping that Uriah would have marital relations with his wife and believe the baby to be his own. Uriah, however, was a soldier of honor. Instead of going home, he slept at the palace entrance. Uriah didn't want to sleep with his wife while his fellow soldiers were camped and awaiting battle.

David sought another method to cover up his actions and invited Uriah to dinner hoping that Uriah would get so drunk that he would set honor aside and go home to his wife. The plan backfired. Even though he was drunk, Uriah slept at the palace entrance once again.

David was desperate. If he couldn't get Uriah to sleep with his wife, then he would just have Uriah killed. He wrote a letter to Joab asking him to put Uriah on the front lines and had the gall to ask Uriah to deliver the letter. Uriah, being the man of honor he was, never read it. He died in the battle. David was relieved. The problem was solved. After the mourning period was over, David sent for Bathsheba and brought her to the palace. She gave birth to his son.

Sin will take you so much further than you ever wanted to go. David's transgression began with laziness in staying home when he should have been at the battlefield with his men. David's laziness led to lust which led to deception and eventually murder. David didn't seem to feel any remorse for his actions. (2nd Samuel 11)

God was angry at what David had done and sent Nathan the prophet with a story to tell David.

"There were two men in a certain town. One was rich, and one was poor. The rich man owned a great many sheep and cattle. The poor man owned nothing but one little lamb he had bought. He raised that little lamb, and it grew up with his children. It ate from the man's own plate and drank from his cup. He cuddled it in his arms like a baby daughter. One day a guest arrived at the home of the rich man. But instead of killing an animal from his own flock or herd, he took the poor man's lamb and killed it and prepared it for his guest."

(2 Samuel 12:1-4)

David became angry when he heard this story and felt that the rich man needed a new attitude. He assumed the story was true and quickly passed judgment upon the man. We often try to assuage our own guilty consciences by passing judgment on someone else.

"As surely as the Lord lives,' he vowed, 'any man who would do such a thing deserves to die! He must repay four lambs to the poor man for the one he stole and for having no pity." (2nd Samuel 12:5-6)

David knew that restitution must take place for the offense. He was appalled by the lack of pity the rich man showed. He conveniently ignored his own lack of pity for what he had done to Uriah. David was ready to pass judgment on the rich man who had no pity, not realizing that he was that very man. Imagine David's surprise when Nathan declared, "You are that man!" Nathan knew that the only way to get David to see his sin was to shock him.

It's easy to see others as the problem instead of ourselves.

Jesus said, *"Why worry about a speck in your friend's eye when you have a log in your own? How can you think of saying, 'Friend, let me help you get rid of that speck in your eye, when you can't see past the log in your own eye? Hypocrite!" (Luke 6:41-42)*

We like to be the victim. We blame others for our problems.

I lost my job because the boss was a jerk. He was so

unreasonable with me.

I didn't do my homework because my mom grounded me from the computer.

The relationship ending was not my fault. I'm a nice person. My boyfriend was a jerk.

I lost my temper because he provoked me.

I robbed that man because I was raised in a bad environment. My dad was a bad influence.

We don't like to take responsibility for our own actions. It's much easier to be the victim and cry, "It's not my fault!" We blame our parents, our siblings, our friends, our mates, our bosses, and our co-workers. Yet, we are never to blame. We are innocent victims. We are good at the blame game. It is always someone else's fault!

The blame game is nothing new. In fact, it began with Adam and Eve. After they both ate the forbidden fruit and hid in shame for their nakedness, God confronted them.

"Who told you that you were naked?' the Lord God asked. 'Have you eaten from the tree whose fruit I commanded you not to eat?

The man replied, 'It was the woman You gave me who gave me the fruit, and I ate it.'

Then the Lord God asked the woman, 'What have you done?'

'The serpent deceived me,' she replied. 'That's why I ate it." (Genesis 3:11-13)

Adam blamed the woman. Eve blamed the snake. Neither took responsibility for their own actions. In their minds, they were the victims. It wasn't their fault. In fact, Adam went so far as to blame God. *"It was the woman You gave me who gave me the fruit."* This is classic behavior: minimize your guilt by making someone else look bad.

God wants us to take responsibility for ourselves. He doesn't want us to blame others for our problems.

"Remember, when you are being tempted, do not say, 'God is tempting me.' God is never tempted to do wrong, and He never tempts anyone else. Temptation comes from our own desires, which entice us and drag us away. These desires give birth to sinful actions." (James 1:13-15)

When Nathan confronted David about his sin, David declared, *"I have sinned against the Lord."* (2nd Samuel 12:13). The first step toward forgiveness is to accept personal responsibility. Who are you blaming for your problems? Whose attitude are you praying that God will change? Who are you asking God to move from your life?

"Why worry about a speck in your friend's eye when you have a log in your own? How can you think of saying, 'Friend, let me help you get rid of that speck in your eye, when you can't see past the log in your own eye? Hypocrite! First get rid of the log in your own eye; then you will see well enough to deal with the speck in your friend's eye" (Luke 6:41-42)

Chapter 11: Grace

I am always looking for object lessons to teach the boys. I had an opportunity one day to teach Matt about grace when he was three years old. Matt and I were sharing a Gatorade after playing outside in the hot, summer heat. I poured Matt's portion into a small cup for him. Matt then dumped it onto the kitchen floor and smiled as the Gatorade formed a sticky, blue puddle. I sent Matt to his room to time out and cleaned up his mess.

When Matt came out of time out, he immediately picked up his empty cup and said, "All gone!"

"Yes," I replied. "You poured yours on the floor."

He held out his cup and said, "Please!"

"You poured yours on the floor, remember? The rest of the bottle is mine!" I told him.

Matt held out his cup once more and said, "Please, I listen!"

That is when it hit me. This was an opportunity to teach Matt about grace.

"You don't deserve any more Gatorade because you

poured yours on the floor, but I am going to show you grace and share some of mine with you."

Matt beamed as he gave me a huge hug. "Thank you!" he declared. "Thank you for showing me grace!"

I realize that this is a small picture of what grace looks like. However, showing grace to others means giving them another chance when they don't deserve it. We show grace to people when they have messed up simply because that is what God does for us each and every day. God doesn't write us off when we make mistakes! In fact, God's mercy is so much bigger than any mistake we have ever made!

Have you ever felt like you have poured too much Gatorade on the floor in God's eyes? Have you made too many mistakes? Would God ever want you – a drug addict, an alcoholic, a thief, an adulterer, a liar, a betrayer, a murderer? Are you too far gone for God to save?

Peter must have felt like that. He was one of Jesus's closest friends. Yet, Peter deserted and even denied knowing Him when Jesus needed a friend the most. Peter let self-preservation stand in the way of his friendship with Jesus. He was deeply ashamed of himself. Peter had been too self-confident in his own abilities. He had proudly declared,

"Even if everyone else deserts You, I will never desert You." (Matthew 26:33)

Jesus knew what was going to happen and replied,

"I tell you the truth, Peter – this very night, before the rooster crows, you will deny three times that you even

know Me." (Matthew 26:34)

Peter was hurt by Jesus's words. Why didn't Jesus believe his loyalty? He insisted,

"No! Even if I have to die with You, I will never deny You!" (Matthew 26:35)

Peter had good intentions. He loved Jesus. Peter never wanted to hurt Him. He thought he was strong enough to face whatever happened. However, he became afraid when Jesus was arrested.

"Meanwhile, Peter was sitting outside in the courtyard. A servant girl came over and said to him, 'You were one of those with Jesus the Galilean.' But Peter denied it in front of everyone.

'I don't know what you're talking about,' he said.

Later, out by the gate, another servant girl noticed him and said to those standing around, 'This man was with Jesus of Nazareth.'

Again Peter denied it, this time with an oath. 'I don't even know this man,' he said.

A little later some of the other bystanders came over to Peter and said, 'You must be one of them; we can tell by your Galilean accent.'

Peter swore, 'A curse on me if I'm lying – I don't know the man!'

And immediately the rooster crowed. Suddenly Jesus's words flashed through Peter's mind: 'Before the rooster crows, you will deny three times that you even know Me.' And he went away, weeping bitterly."

(Matthew 26:69-75)

Sometimes, our friends desert us when we need them the most. We feel angry, hurt, and unforgiving. We want to write those people off and never see them again. We think, "Why should I show them grace? They don't deserve it!"

Peter wept because he was ashamed of his actions. This boastful, prideful, self-sufficient man had done just as Jesus had predicted. It is bad enough when we let someone down. The feeling is even worse when we know that person knew in advance that we would. Jesus knew Peter better than Peter knew himself. Peter's story could have ended there. When Jesus rose from the grave, he had every right to be angry at Peter after what he had done. Peter had proved that he was a coward. He didn't deserve a second chance.

I am thankful that God does not respond to situations like we do. Jesus had every right to write Peter off, yet He didn't. Peter deserved condemnation, but God offered him grace. When the women visited Jesus's tomb at sunrise on Sunday morning they saw an angel.

"Don't be alarmed. You are looking for Jesus of Nazareth, who was crucified. He isn't here! He is risen from the dead! Look, this is where they laid His body. Now go and tell His disciples, including Peter, that Jesus is going ahead of you to Galilee. You will see Him there, just as He told you before He died." (Mark 16: 6-7)

The angel specifically told the women to tell "His disciples, including Peter" that Jesus was going to meet them in Galilee. Peter wasn't excluded because of his denial. Of all the disciples that could have been mentioned by name, Peter was the only one listed. Peter had denied Jesus three times and deserted Him in His time of need. Peter had walked away in shame with tears streaming down his face. Jesus took the time to single Peter out through this message to show him that He still considered him a friend. Jesus wasn't mad at him. He didn't write Peter off. Jesus chose to show Peter grace, forgiveness, and mercy.

"And within the hour they were on their way back to Jerusalem. There they found the eleven disciples and the others who had gathered with them, who said, 'The Lord has really risen! He appeared to Peter!"(Luke 24:33-34)

Imagine how Peter must have felt. Our God is a God of second chances! God loves imperfect people who have messed up and failed. He didn't write Peter off for his denial and desertion. God didn't write David off for killing Bathsheba's husband (2nd Samuel 11). Jacob wasn't written off for his deceit (Genesis 27).

God knows everything about you. He knows what you have said, done, and even thought. You can't keep your deepest secrets that you are ashamed of from God. Are you bothered by that? Do you ever wonder why God doesn't just write you off since He knows how imperfect you are? People write us off for making mistakes, but God doesn't! He loves us too much!

Peter had not messed up too much for God to use him, even though he surely felt that he had.

"After breakfast Jesus asked Simon Peter, 'Simon, son of John, do you love Me more than these?'

'Yes, Lord,' Peter replied, 'You know I love You.'

Jesus repeated the question: 'Simon, son of John, 'do you love Me?'

'Yes, Lord,' Peter said, 'You know I love You.'

'Then take care of My sheep,' Jesus said.

A third time he asked Him, 'Simon, son of John, do you love Me?'

Peter was hurt that Jesus asked the question a third time. He said, 'Lord, You know everything. You know that I love You.'

Jesus said, 'Then feed My sheep." (John 21:15-17)

Peter had proudly claimed to be more loyal than the other disciples and to love Jesus so much that he would die for him (Matthew 26:33-35). Yet, Jesus knew Peter better than Peter knew himself and accurately predicted Peter's three denials. Jesus now asked about Peter's love three times while commissioning him to be His shepherd. Jesus wasn't through with Peter!

I once had a falling out with my prayer partner, Hannah. I had become very insecure and needy in that friendship while tossing more of my baggage in her car than she had room for. I was on a self-pity journey and made many comments to her that came across as critical and hurtful. Hurt people hurt others, and I took it out on her. Insecurity also breeds insecurity. The friendship became so unhealthy that Hannah decided to write me off. She couldn't take anymore. I was devastated to say the least. I had never meant to hurt her, but I had. Peter never meant to hurt Jesus, but he did.

Our friendship was over. We both had said some hurtful things to each other. I felt so much shame, but there was nothing I could do to fix the friendship. She had blocked my phone number. We didn't speak for a year, then I attended a women's retreat that I knew she would probably be at. Remembering the last angry words she had said to me, I was full of anxiety at the possibility of seeing her there. Fear of rejection ruled me at that time, and I didn't want to go through that again. I was overcome with shame. "What if I run into her, and she still hates me?" I was afraid to face her. I could understand the shame Peter must have felt to have hurt his closest friend.

I began praying selfish prayers. *"God, this is a huge place, and there are going to be a lot of people here. Please let our paths not cross!"* Shame makes you want to avoid a situation.

I do believe that God has a sense of humor because he made me face my giant the very first day. We both ended up being asked to pray together over guests entering the facility.

Hannah was being her usual nice self and gave me a hug before we started praying. My thoughts were:

"Wow! We must be pretending here because we have this huge unresolved issue between us. Why does God want US to pray together for other people? This is absolutely crazy!"

I didn't know what to do since guests were coming in the door, so I began to pray together with her for them all the while thinking,

"This is totally awkward! I prayed to avoid her, not

to pray with her!"

After a few hours of praying and small talk, we each went our separate ways at the retreat with the unresolved issue between us. Hannah was outwardly nice, but I didn't know where her heart was. My stomach was tied in knots all weekend. Every message was about making amends. The burden to apologize was heavy on my heart, yet I was ruled by the fear of rejection. What if she didn't accept my apology? What if she really was just outwardly pretending things were fine? I was too chicken to find out. I knew I had screwed up that friendship. I just didn't think I could handle the burden of more shame, so I took the coward's approach. I tried my best to avoid her. Peter and I have a lot in common.

I stayed up for hours the final night praying,

"God, I am so willing to admit I was wrong. I am willing to take all the blame, but God don't make me approach her first! I don't have the courage to face this kind of rejection! Let her come to me and make the first move!"

I prayed that prayer many times, but I never had peace over what I was praying about because I sensed God telling ME to make that first move. The opportunity arose the next morning when she sat on the same row as me. I sat glued to the pew as I felt God saying,

"Now is your opportunity. Go! Ask her if you can talk afterwards."

Have you ever tried to run from what God wants you to do? Just like He did with Jonah, He will bring that opportunity back around. I had tried to avoid

Hannah all weekend out of shame. Now, she was sitting on the same pew as me. There was no doubt in my mind that was a God thing! As everyone stood to sing the lyrics to "How Great is Our God", I made my way over to her. She smiled at me with a questioning look in her eyes as I approached. "Can we talk for like five minutes after this?" I asked. "Sure!" she responded.

I spent the next hour and a half praying,

"God, this is Your doing here. You have given me this opportunity to make things right finally. Please give me the words to say and the courage to face her rejection and anger!"

I knew that I deserved her rejection and anger. I just didn't want to face it. I planned on apologizing for my insecure words and behavior and then running out of the chapel as fast I could before she could respond. However, as soon as I finished apologizing, she looked at me and apologized as well before I could flee. We then sat there for a while and talked. Hannah even mentioned about being friends again and asked how I felt about that. I stared at her in shock. I had carried the burden of guilt and shame over my actions for a year and was prepared to do so for the rest of my life. I didn't deserve her forgiveness or her friendship. Yet, she offered me both. Hannah exemplified to me what Jesus did to Peter. She showed me grace!

Grace is God giving us what we don't deserve. Grace is not earned; it is a gift. There was nothing I could do to earn Hannah's forgiveness or her friendship. We can't earn God's forgiveness either. Forgiveness is a gift through grace.

"God saved you by His grace when you believed. And you can't take credit for this; it is a gift from God. Salvation is not a reward for the good things we have done, so none of us can boast about it." (Ephesians 2:8-9)

The Bible is quite clear on forgiveness.

"Get rid of all bitterness, rage, anger, harsh words, and slander, as well as all types of evil behavior. Instead, be kind to each other, tenderhearted, forgiving one another, just as God through Christ has forgiven you." (Ephesians 4:32)

"If you forgive those who sin against you, your heavenly Father will forgive you. But if you refuse to forgive others, your Father will not forgive your sins." (Matthew 6:14)

Forgive others because you have been forgiven. No matter what you have done or where you are in life, you are not too messed up for God to save! You may have experienced people who have given up on you, but God will not write you off. Peter experienced God's gift of grace and forgiveness, and you can too.

"May you have the power to understand, as all God's people should, how wide, how long, how high, and how deep His love is." (Ephesians 3:18)

Chapter 12: Making the Impossible Possible!

God sometimes speaks to us through other people, yet we try not to hear it because the idea seems so absurd to us. That happens to have been the case with me. About a year ago, friends and acquaintances began to occasionally suggest that I publish a book of my writings that I share via e-mails and on Facebook. I laughed it off at first. I enjoy sharing my heart and my experiences in the hope that others may be blessed. I pray that those who read my words may be lifted by crying with me, laughing with me, or at me as the case may be. However, I have NEVER considered myself a writer.

Those occasional suggestions slowly began to come more frequently. At least one or two different people a month for five months told me that I should write a book or asked when I am going to publish my book. I still laughed it off. "I'm not a writer," I replied each time. As I continued to share my "God moments" and spiritual analogies via e-mail and on Facebook, the suggestions to write a book began coming once a week, sometimes twice in one week, by even more people. Although some friends and acquaintances still advised me to write a book, most of the suggestions came from people that I didn't know very well.

The frequency of these suggestions and the fact that they were coming from numerous people led me to consider that it just might be God speaking to me through them. As I watched Matt finally stop stalling at the midway point of the climbing wall and reach the top, I actually considered myself stalled out on a spiritual climbing wall.

"Hey God, I share my 'journal' on Facebook and through e-mail. That's good enough, isn't it? Why would you want me to publish it? Besides, what do I know about writing a book?"

Fear. I know it quite well. All of us have experienced it. We all fear different things. I recently heard a seventy-five year old woman share her story of overcoming the fear of rejection at the age of seventy-two. God had given her talent as a songwriter, singer, and painter. Yet, she was too paralyzed by fear for most of her life to share that talent with others. At the age of seventy-two, she overcame the fear of rejection and began combining her art and music into wonderful presentations to glorify God. Fear is something we all experience no matter what our age is.

I happen to be terrified of rejection. The fear of being rejected hindered me for years from selling my photography. God gave me a talent to capture beauty with a camera. I kept that talent to myself because I was too afraid that my work wasn't good enough. "It will never sell," I thought, "so why bother trying." Fear of rejection inhibited me to speak in front of groups of people and lead Bible studies. It prevented me from making phone calls without writing out scripts first.

Yet, God has given me the strength to do all of those things now. Why was I still stalling midway on a spiritual climbing wall when God was using numerous people to tell me to write a book?

It was interesting question to ponder. Meanwhile, I asked for one more sign.

"Okay God, if this is what You truly want me to do, then let two people suggest this to me in one day!"

The suggestions had been coming frequently at that point, but I had never experienced two suggestions in one day by two different people.

I went to a small Baptist church the next morning. In the foyer, I was approached by the senior pastor who immediately said, "I read your blog (referring to a recent God moment I had posted on Facebook). You need to publish your journal!" As we were finishing up our conversation, the secretary of that church approached me stating the same thing as I stared in wonder. God had just given me my sign!

I have learned that a lot of times when God calls us to do something, it is not something we want to do. In fact, a lot of times the very thought of doing it seems so absurd to us that we try to ignore it or run from it. I knew nothing about writing and publishing a book. This was definitely my own personal Nineveh that God seemed to be leading me to. I decided to stop telling God, "This is good enough," as I stalled at a comfortable point on the spiritual climbing wall. I chose instead to follow His leading.

Fear does not come from God (2nd Timothy 1:7). Fear is the devil trying to keep you from doing what

God wants you to do. Moses understood fear. He was born when the Israelites were slaves in Egypt. Pharaoh was concerned because the number of Israelites was multiplying. He decreed that all of their baby boys were to be tossed into the Nile River. Moses's mother hid him in a basket among the reeds of the banks of the Nile where he was found by Pharaoh's daughter who adopted him as her own. Moses grew up in the king's palace and was considered a son of Pharaoh, but surely he must have had a fear of becoming a slave like his own people.

Moses went to visit the slaves one day and was appalled at how hard they were forced to work. He saw an Egyptian beating a slave and took action. He killed the Egyptian and hid his body in the sand. Moses was afraid that Pharaoh would find out what had happened, so he fled to Midian where he started a family. The former Prince of Egypt became a shepherd in the wilderness. As he was tending to the flock one day, God appeared to him in a burning bush and told him,

"I have certainly seen the oppression of My people in Egypt. I have heard their cries of distress because of their harsh slave drivers. Yes, I am aware of their suffering. So I have come down to rescue them from the power of the Egyptians and lead them out of Egypt into their own fertile and spacious land." (Exodus3:7-8)

"Now go, for I am sending you to Pharaoh. You must lead my people Israel out of Egypt." (Exodus 3:10)

Moses was insecure and protested,

"Who am I to appear before Pharaoh? Who am I to lead the people of Israel out of Egypt?" (Exodus 3:11)

God called Moses to do the impossible – to lead the oppressed slaves of Israel back to this very site. Moses had to have thought, "Why me? Doesn't God know that I am insecure? Doesn't God know that I am afraid of Pharaoh?" Moses had doubts and fears of his own ability to lead the people and was afraid of their reception to him.

"What if they won't believe me or listen to Me? What if they say, 'The Lord never appeared to you?' (Exodus 4:1)

"O Lord, I'm not very good with words. I never have been, and I'm not now, even though You have spoken to me. I get tongue-tied, and my words get tangled." (Exodus 4:10)

"Lord, please! Send anyone else." (Exodus 4:13)

God became angry at Moses's objections and decided to let his brother, Aaron, be Moses's mouthpiece. Even with God and Aaron by his side, Moses still suffered from a lack of self-esteem. When God told Moses to tell Pharaoh everything that He had told him, Moses still protested,

"I can't do it! I'm such a clumsy speaker! Why should Pharaoh listen to me?" (Exodus 6:30)

Do Moses's words sound familiar? I said several similar statements to God when I felt Him leading me to become a speaker.

"God, don't You know that I suffer from social anxiety and that I'm not good with words? Don't make me do this! Don't make me embarrass myself!"

"What if nobody listens to me when I speak? What if they "boo" me off the stage? I'm not a speaker. Who am I to speak at these churches and events?"

What I didn't understand and what Moses didn't understand at the time was that God has the power to make the impossible possible. As Paul stated in Ephesians,

"Now all glory to God, who is able, through His mighty power at work within us, to accomplish infinitely more than we might ask or think." (Ephesians 3:20)

God changes us from the inside out and transforms each of us into a whole new person. Transformation doesn't happen overnight, but as we grow in our relationship with God, He begins to change us inwardly. God changes the way we think and what we believe which slowly alters who we are and who we will become. Your past and even your present do not have to define you. God can and will change you in ways that you never could have imagined! He goes big while we think small. I never dreamed of doing any of the things I do today such as public speaking, leading Bible studies, or volunteering at events because I was too hindered by fear. I was shy and insecure. I suffered from low self-esteem and poor self-image. Yet, God made what was absolutely impossible in my life possible!

It has never been my desire to be an author. I'm not sure why God wanted me to write this book. I don't know God's reasons for this book. However, I have sensed His leading and presence during this whole journey. I refuse to let fear hold me back from taking a step into the unknown writer's world. God has a plan and that's good enough for me. As the title of this book states, "It's a God Thing!"

What is God calling you to do right now that you are trying to talk your way out of? Are you hindered with fear over something God has asked you to do? Are you worried about being rejected or embarrassed? Are you begging God, "Send someone else, please!"? Are you thinking small and giving God excuses of why you can't do something when God wants to make an impossibility a possibility in your life?

"For God has not given us a spirit of fear and timidity, but of power, love, and self-discipline."

(2nd Timothy 1:7)

(Nothing is impossible with God!)

Part 4: Epilogue

Chapter 1: Seeing God in the Pain

My mother passed away during the editing stages of this book. She had suffered from vascular dementia caused by multiple mini-strokes for several years. As I sat by her bedside in the hospice room and watched her grimace in pain, I felt anger toward God for not relieving her suffering. I begged God to either do a miracle of healing or to take her life. Sometimes, God doesn't answer our prayers right away. She passed away seven long days after entering in-hospital hospice.

The death of a loved one can be a lonely time. My friends and church family were not there for me in the way that I needed and wanted. In the midst of that sadness, anger, hurt, and pain, I wrote a song entitled, "I See God in the Pain". God was there despite how alone, angry, sad, and hurt I felt. He will never abandon us in our time of need. God didn't abandon me, and He didn't abandon my mom.

She clung to her hope in Christ despite her circumstances. Mama was unable to communicate. However, my aunt placed a small, wooden cross in her hand. My mom held on to that cross for several days until she died. She never let go of it and kept her fingers clutched around it. I like to think that wooden cross stood as a reminder to her of the hope to come. She saw God in the pain!

I pray that you will be blessed by the words of my song, "I See God in the Pain".

I See God in the Pain

© Tonya Hance

When I walk through the darkest valley
And feel like a ship tossed at sea,
My faith is tested and bested
By the waves that overtake me.

When darkness surrounds me
And troubles begin to rain,
I feel discouraged and yearn for some hope
To know God is there in the pain.

(chorus)Yet, I see God in the mountains before me
All covered white with snow
When my faith crumbles like leaves in the dead of the night
And morning comes so slow.
I see God in the desert canyons
Barren and lonely as can be.
Although I didn't choose to walk this valley,
I can have victory.
I see God
In the Rain.
I see God
In the Pain.

When the struggles of life surround me
And my heart aches with pain,
I can't see the sun or the morning to come
In the midst of the pouring rain.

When my faith is shaken
And trials seem too big to bear,
I feel alone in the valley
And wonder if anyone cares.

(chorus)Yet, I see God in the mountains before me
All covered white with snow
When my faith crumbles like leaves in the dead of the night
And morning comes so slow.
I see God in the desert canyons
Barren and lonely as can be.
Although I didn't choose to walk this valley,
I can have victory.
I see God
In the Rain.
I see God
In the Pain.

Chapter 2: The Road to Salvation

Thank you for taking the time to read this book. If you picked it up out of curiosity and do not know Jesus Christ as your personal Lord and Savior or have a relationship with Him, I would like to share what is known as the "Roman Road" with you. The Roman Road, taken from the book of Romans in the Bible, provides a map for salvation and eternal relationship with God.

It is important to follow a map when hiking in the wilderness. Without Jesus, one is wandering in a spiritual wilderness. There are many paths, but only one path leads to God. (Matthew 7:13-14)

Step One: Acknowledge God as Creator. God has provided evidence of His existence through Creation. There are no excuses for those who deny Him.

"For ever since the world was created, people have seen the earth and sky. Through everything God made, they can clearly see His invisible qualities – His eternal power and divine nature. So they have no excuse for not knowing God." (Romans 1: 20)

Step Two: Realize and admit that you are a sinner in need of forgiveness and grace.

"For everyone has sinned; we all fall short of God's glorious standard." (Romans 3:23)

Step Three: Believe that God sent His Son, Jesus Christ, to pay the penalty of our sins.

"But God showed His great love for us by sending Christ to die for us while we were still sinners." (Romans 5:8)

Step Four: Recognize that you will die without Jesus. However, if you repent of your sins and accept Jesus as your Lord and Savior, you will live eternally.

"For the wages of sin is death, but the free gift of God is eternal life through Jesus Christ our Lord." (Romans 6:23)

Step Five: You will be saved when you confess that Jesus Christ is Lord and believe in your heart that God raised Him from the dead.

"If you confess with your mouth that Jesus is Lord and believe in your heart that God raised Him from the dead, you will be saved." (Romans 10:9)

Step Six: Call upon the name of the Lord, and you will be saved.

"For everyone who calls on the name of the Lord will be saved." (Romans 10:13)

Step Seven: Make Jesus Christ the Lord of your life today.

"For everything comes from Him and exists by His power and is intended for His glory. All glory to Him forever! Amen." (Romans 11:36)

If you would like Jesus's gift of eternal life:

1. Tell Him that you are a sinner.

2. Tell Him that you recognize that you cannot save yourself.

3. Tell Him that You believe that Jesus Christ paid your sin debt on the cross with his blood.

4. Confess Jesus as Lord.

5. Pray a prayer such as the following.

"Lord Jesus, I turn from my sins to You. I confess that I am a sinner, and I am sorry. I need a Savior. I know that I cannot save myself. I confess you as Lord. I believe that God raised you from the dead, and I trust You to save me. I ask You to forgive my sin and come into my heart. I trust You as my Savior and receive You as my Lord. Thank You, Jesus, for saving me. Help me to live for you. Amen."

If you have prayed that prayer, please share the good news and connect with fellow Christians. Remember, God does not intend for us to be Christian lone rangers.

www.ingramcontent.com/pod-product-compliance
Lightning Source LLC
Chambersburg PA
CBHW071959040426
42447CB00009B/1411
9780692590898